STILL
LOOKIN' FOR LOVE

"When my life flashes before my eyes... it'll be worth watching."

- Johnny Lee

Johnny Lee
Still Lookin' for Love
The Autobiography

© copyright 2017 England Media
102 Rachels Ct Hendersonville TN 37075
(615) 804-0361
englandmedia@yahoo.com

ISBN 978-0-9986367-0-2

All rights reserved under International Copyright Law contents and/or cover may not be reproduced in whole or in part in any form without the express written consent of the Publisher

Editor: Lindsey McNealy
Cover Design/Layout: Paula Underwood Winters

Printed in the United States of America

If you like Johnny Lee's autobiography, you'll love his cookbook "Chef Boy 'R' Lee"! You can find Johnny's cookbook, CDs and other merchandise, along with all of his tour dates at johnnyleemusic.com

DEDICATION

I dedicate this book to anyone who's ever crossed paths with me throughout my life. And if we haven't crossed paths yet, hopefully one day we will.

To my fans, my friends and my family… you are the ones who helped me make all of these memories.

I thank everyone who has ever bought a Johnny Lee record or a concert ticket. You are the ones who have made my entire career possible.

I am living proof that dreams really can come true… if you just stick with it.

FOREWORD

For the past ten years, Johnny Lee has been saying he was going to write his autobiography…but he had to wait until Mickey Gilley died first. Well, I guess Johnny finally got tired of waiting. I'm still here!

Johnny Lee is a fabulous performer and entertainer. You won't find anybody any better. Johnny is a very good singer. He's a good stylist. He's a great storyteller. And boy, do we have a lot of stories!

Since my first success came a few years before his did, I'm sure there were times when he might have been a little bit jealous. But he handled it very well. And I know that he used me as a kind of motivation, as he said, 'If my buddy Mickey can do it, I can too!' I also know that he was happy for me, when my hit records started coming. And I was just as thrilled for him when his hits started.

Johnny and I were able to see the world. And we were paid to see it! We lived through a truly magical time. We worked very hard, but we also played hard.

We were friends when we were both flat broke. We had nothing but our dreams. And we were friends when we were living like kings, on top of the world. And most importantly, we are friends today… closer than ever.

I am honored to have spent most of my life working with Johnny. It's been a great ride.

Mickey Gilley

Johnny Lee is one of my closest friends.

When he first told me he was writing this book, I said, "I know you aren't putting everything in it!"

Johnny yelled, "Yes I am!"

I just shook my head and said, "Oh Lord, we are all in trouble."

I actually remember the very first time I met Johnny. I had a local band in Texas and I had had a few hit records at that time, and I was booked to play at Gilley's.

Johnny came out, and looked at my bus. He said, "One of these days, I'm gonna have one of these." He then gave me an album that he had done. It was on an independent label.

I will never forget how he said "I'm going to get me a bus one of these days". And just a short time later, his hits started coming, and soon enough, he had a nicer bus than I did!

I knew Johnny before anyone had ever heard of him, then I watched him become a household name, and one of the biggest stars in country music. And through it all, he has never changed. He's still the same great guy that he was back when he was dreaming of getting his own bus.

Johnny is one the best showmen that I've ever been around. When he does a show, he really entertains people. He is one of the absolute funniest guys I've ever met. He and I have the same sense of humor, and he is my golfing buddy. So get ready for some very funny stories about our times on the golf course!

Johnny is my friend. We are very tight. I was actually in the hospital with him when he was coming out of his cancer surgery. I'm sure he'll tell you about the special gift that I had waiting for him.

Johnny tells you what he thinks. I like that. He is so honest, and you will soon find that out as you read through this book. Oh Lord, we are all in trouble!

Moe Bandy

Moe Bandy

STILL
Lookin' For Love

JOHNNY LEE

The Autobiography
With Scot England

CONTENTS

Foreword by Mickey Gilley 7
Foreword by Moe Bandy 8
Chapter One – October, 2016 15
Chapter Two – A Star is Born…In Texas City……........................17
Chapter Three – Finding Love…and the Roadrunners….............27
Chapter Four - So You Want To See the World? 33
Chapter Five - Meeting Mickey…………………………….............39
Chapter Six - Gilley's 45
Chapter Seven - Urban Cowboy 53
Chapter Eight – A Ride Wilder Than a Mechanical Bull 59
Chapter Nine - Charlene 67
Chapter Ten - Ricky Dies…and Sherwood Lives 75
Chapter Eleven - Cherish 85
Chapter Twelve - Debbie 91
Chapter Thirteen - Colon Cancer…A Real Pain in the Ass 97
Chapter Fourteen - My Country Music Friends 101
Chapter Fifteen – Johnny Lee the Second 117
Chapter Sixteen – Losing Johnny 121
Chapter Seventeen – Connor 129
Chapter Eighteen – Your Toupee Really Sucks 131
Chapter Nineteen – Entertaining 141
Chapter Twenty – Fore! 145
Chapter Twenty One – Just The Good Ole Boys 151
Chapter Twenty Two – Adults Only! 159
Chapter Twenty Three – Family Time 175
Chapter Twenty Four – Hit Songs 183
Chapter Twenty Five – The Future 189
Chapter Twenty Six – Parting Song 195

Johnny Lee

Saying Hello to my grandson Wyatt.

CHAPTER ONE

October, 2016 - Nashville

Welcome to the world, little Wyatt. I have been waiting for you… my first grandchild… for a long time! You are so tiny. And my love for you is so huge. Thank you, God, for letting my grandson be healthy.

Wyatt Rein Christopher. I think that's a wonderful name for a great little boy. Wyatt, your mom says that she chose your name because it means, "Little warrior, guided by Christ". I pray that you will be guided by Christ through your life, and I sure hope that you are a little warrior… to be born into this family, you will need to be one!

Little guy, I have had quite a year. I turned 70 years old. My first grandchild was born. And I have been writing my life story.

Wyatt, I wonder what your reaction will be when you read my book. Hopefully, you'll say, "Wow, my grandpa was pretty cool! And he lived an amazing life." There might be one or two things in here that will surprise, or even embarrass you, but I hope that you'll be able to say, "My grandpa wasn't perfect. He never claimed to be. But he had a great heart, and he loved everyone. He was always honest, and he always told the truth."

As I hold you in my hands, Wyatt, I see my future. And as I look forward to what's ahead in the years to come, I think this is a good time to take one more look back at the past 70 years. My grandson Wyatt… have I got a story for you!

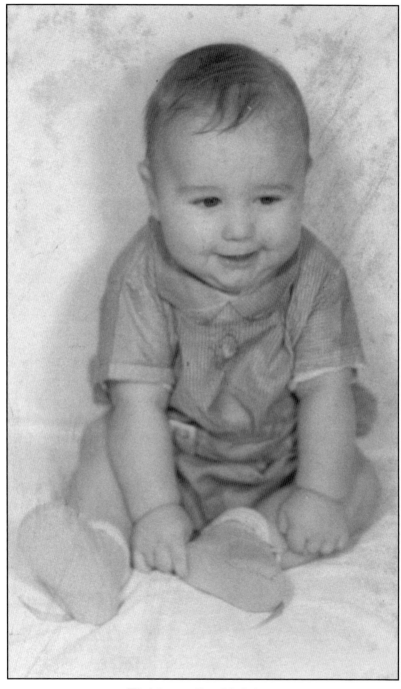

Eight month old Johnny

CHAPTER TWO

A Star is Born... In Texas City

"I remember the day I was born. They circumcised me and it hurt so damn bad, I couldn't walk for a year."

– Johnny Lee

I was born in Texas City, Texas on July 3, 1946. The next day, everyone set off fireworks, and I'm sure I thought at the time they were celebrating me!

My dad walked out on my mother the day he found out she was pregnant with me. He told her he couldn't stand being around pregnant women. And then he just left her. He said, "I will see you when it's over with." Who says that? "When it's over with."

And he kept his word. Dad came back around when I was almost a year old, but he told mom that he would leave again if she ever got pregnant again. But mom wasn't going to take any more of his crap. She wouldn't let him come back. She told him goodbye, and sure enough, he never came back.

When I was less than a year old, it wasn't just fireworks going off in my hometown. The great Texas City refinery explosion happened on April 16, 1947. You really had to have been in Texas at the time to comprehend what a huge disaster this was.

More than 580 people were killed. More than 5,000 were injured. 63 people were never identified, and 113 were simply listed as missing, because no identifiable body parts were ever found. More than 500 homes were completely destroyed, and hundreds more were damaged.

I was still a baby, but this was so horrific that I can actually remember it. I can remember chaos. When the explosion occurred, my aunt Mary Lou had tried to cover me to protect me. There is a history book about the explosion, and my mom and I were both listed as being killed. Mom was supposed to be at work that day, but for some reason, she didn't go. So, she was listed as missing when the explosion happened.

The house that I grew up in in Texas City was located in a housing addition called Snug Harbor. I thought our house was a mansion, but I actually went back to look at it years later, and it couldn't have been more than 800 square feet. My grandpa, my grandma, my mother, my aunt, me, and my uncle Jimmy all lived there.

My mom's sister, Mary Lou Miller, was like a second mother to me. Mom had to work all the time after my Dad left her, so Mary Lou took care of me. She really babied me, and kind of treated me like a little toy doll. She was a wonderful woman.

As the town of Texas City was still trying to recover from the refinery explosion, my mom remarried one year later. And my life was rocked again… by the birth of my brother Lynn.

Up until then, I had been the center of attention in our family, but when the new baby came along, everyone's attention shifted over to him. And even at the age of two, I could see the writing on the wall. So I ran away. I ran through a field behind our house, but my family found me and brought me back home. Two days later, I started a fire in our kitchen. I caught the kitchen on fire. It seemed like I would do almost anything to get a little attention… still do.

My Grandpa Wilson worked in the oil refineries. He was my hero. I loved that man so much.

Every time he would go anywhere, even just to work, Grandpa would bring me back a present. He would always bring me a piece of candy, or maybe a yoyo.

One time, he forgot to bring me something, but he reached into his bag and pulled out one of those little coil door stops. You know, the little thing that you screw into a baseboard by your door so the door doesn't hit the wall. It has a spring and goes *"D-woing!"* when you flick it with your finger.

I thought that that was the neatest gift I had ever gotten in my life! I played with it for hours.

Grandpa Wilson passed away when I was on my first deployment in Vietnam. My CO came and told me that he had died.

My Step-Grandpa Linkey had one lung. He couldn't read or write. We used to sit in his lap and read him the comics. He loved Dagwood, and when he'd start laughing, he would lose his breath, and we'd have to wait until he caught his breath before we could finish reading to him.

My Uncle Jimmy was also cool. I loved hanging out with Uncle Jimmy, but one time he brought a girl over to our house, and he didn't want me around. I was young, and had no idea what they were doing. But he locked me in the closet! From inside, I could hear sounds like someone was hurt. They were moaning and groaning! I fumbled around and happened to find some matches in the closet. And I set it on fire. Luckily, when they smelled smoke, the moaning stopped and they let me out of the closet!

There was a big pole in our front yard. It was actually a pipe of some sort, and I liked to play around it. One day, I was waiting for the ice cream man to come by. I had a buffalo head nickel to pay for my treat, but as I was playing by that pipe, I dropped the nickel way down the hole.

When the ice cream man came by, I told him, "I lost my nickel. Can I have some ice cream today and then pay you tomorrow?" He wouldn't do it.

By the way, the ice cream man had no legs! But that didn't stop him from driving his cart around town. You would hear that ice cream music coming down the street. It kind of freaked me out that he didn't have any legs, but I wanted that ice cream so bad.

I have one more memory about the ice cream guy. When I was really little, my uncle told me that when the ice cream man was playing music on his truck that meant he was all out of ice cream! It didn't take me long to figure that one out.

I was in the first grade when I fell in love with an older woman: my teacher, Miss Star. She was beautiful! Miss Star was there during one of my most embarrassing moments. We were in class, when I suddenly had to go the bathroom… number 2! Miss Star excused me as I ran toward the restroom… an outhouse that was 150 yards away!

I had gotten only about a quarter of the way there, when I started going to the bathroom in my pants. I started running faster, but the outhouse was so far away! By the time I got there, I had crapped all over myself.

I closed the outhouse door behind me and started crying. My mind was racing, trying to figure out what to do. I knew my mother would miss the underwear if I threw them away. So, I cleaned myself up and tried to wash out my underwear. Then, I discovered that they were too wet and still too dirty to put back on. I ended up cramming them into the back pocket of my blue jeans. I went back to class and tried to act like nothing had happened. Even today, when I think of Miss Star, I about crap my pants!

One of my favorite childhood memories is of making homemade ice cream. It was much better than anything that no-legged ice cream man was selling! We'd put in big chunks of sea salt and ice, and turn that crank. We'd turn it until it got hard, and that's when it was good.

We used to pick dewberries. Mom would make dewberry cobbler. And if you put some peaches on your homemade ice cream… oh man, my tongue would beat my brains out trying to get to it. There was also a fig tree outside my window. And I would break off the figs, knock the milk off the end of the vine, and eat those figs.

But when I was nine years old, I traded those figs for cigarettes. I started smoking when I was a kid. I took my first puff and got dizzy, as I stood there trying to smoke a Camel cigarette.

And that would just be the first of tens of thousands of cigarettes that I would smoke.

But my smoking came to an abrupt end one night in Pearland, Texas. I tried to hit a note, and something happened to my vocal chords. I said, "That's it. I quit smoking." I stopped on the spot. It was not even an option. Cigarettes are not going to be the ruler of my life, and they are damn sure not going to stop me from singing. And from that moment on, I have never smoked.

It's a wonder I haven't died from lung cancer just from the smoke at Gilley's all those years. Now, there are so many laws against smoking inside, but there are still nights when I play a place where there is smoking, and it really bothers me. That smoke gets on my clothes, and in my nose and in my mouth. It is horrible for a performer.

My mom's second husband Bill was really a people person. He never met a stranger, and everyone liked him.

But he had just one bad habit. He liked to beat my mom. They would be playing cards with friends, when all of the sudden he would turn to my mom and say, "I just feel like beating the hell out of you." And he would hit her hard. One time, she picked up a heavy glass ash tray and hit him back.

Bill was the father of my brother Lynn and my sister Claudia. Bill loved to fish. He would take my brother Lynn fishing, but I was never invited. I was so envious of Lynn. I wished I had a dad who would do that with me.

One day Bill surprised me, when he said, "Come on, let's all go fishing." I was so excited! We got into his old Ford, and we took off. He was going about 70 miles an hour when he ran into a construction zone, and we had a very bad wreck. The crash actually threw me out of the front windshield! There weren't any seat belts back then, and it's a miracle we all lived through the crash. But I never got to go fishing.

One time, Bill took a pocket knife and stabbed himself in the leg. He really drove that knife down deep into his leg! But he had a wooden leg. He lost his leg when he caught a catfish. For some reason, he had one of his violent outbursts, and kicked the fish. And part of that fish's fin broke off in his foot. His foot ended up getting an infection, and they had to take off his leg in order to save his life.

After one too many beatings, mom divorced Bill, but she wasn't single for long. Her third husband was a dairy farmer named Jim Linkey. That marriage produced my brother Jimmy, and my sisters Janice and Janet. They are twins.

While the names of her husbands may have changed, it seems that my mother would always end up in abusive relationships. I remember the day that Jim took a belt to her, but I was not old enough or big enough to stop it at the time.

I didn't get along with my step dad at all. When I was a kid, he always told me I was going to end up in prison.

When I made it big, he came to see my show, and they made him pay a cover charge to get in. I wasn't about to say anything. I liked that he had to pay to come see me.

I didn't have a real happy childhood. I worked my ass off on our dairy farm near Alta Loma (now Santa Fe), Texas. I was just eight years old when they put me to work!

In our family, if you were a male, you had to start working on the dairy farm when you were eight. We had to get up at 1:30 in the morning. We'd milk cows until 6 am. We'd take a bath in a three-foot aluminum tub. We didn't have any indoor plumbing.

Then, we'd go to school. And as soon as school was over, we'd have to go back to milking the cows until dark.

During the summer, we would have to bale hay and herd cattle. But I did get paid. I made two to three dollars a week. When I got older, I made $5.00 a week. I thought I was rich!

I saved up enough money to buy a new pair of Levi's. You weren't cool unless you were wearing Levi's. For some reason, I wanted to wash my new pants myself. I had never done laundry before. I put a half bottle of bleach in the washer… and I ruined my new Levi's.

We raised our own pork. My step grandma and grandpa Linkey had an old smokehouse, and we would hang meat up in there.

Most days, Grandma would go out and grab a couple chickens. She'd ring their necks, and we'd watch them flop around until they died. We'd clean the feathers off of them, and she'd take them in and cook them. We raised our own beef, grew our own vegetables, and we made our own butter.

You never heard about people getting cancer back then. I still believe that's because of the good and natural food we used to eat.

When I wasn't working on the farm, I was playing baseball. I played little league. I lived for that game! I was a pretty strong kid. Working on the farm made me strong. When I wasn't baling hay, I was carrying 5-gallon buckets of milk, lifting them up all morning and all night. I was a hardworking kid.

One day, the coach asked me to pitch, and I threw the ball over the backstop. But I ended up being a good pitcher. I also played shortstop, and in the outfield. I could always throw the ball from the outfield all the way to home plate.

My step dad made us go to church. He wouldn't go himself, but he wanted us out of the house, so he would make us go. I got saved when I was in Jr. High. My first musical performance was in church. I played the trumpet in a church service. I did "The Old Rugged Cross", and I was so nervous!

When I was herding cattle on our farm, I would pretend I was a singer and I'd sing to the cows. At the time, I wasn't into country music. I was listening to Doo-Wop music, and all the 50s groups. I'd be in the barn milking the cows, as I listened to Elvis and Fats Domino. The only time we'd dial the radio over to a country station is when Grandpa would show up. I was young and dumb, and I just didn't appreciate country music at the time.

One day, I was on a horse, rounding up cattle. Grandpa had 660 acres, and you needed a horse to cover all of that. One day, when I was in junior high school, I was rounding up the cattle by myself. I was a couple miles away from home when the horse threw me. When I fell, I broke my leg.

I can still remember lying there in the pasture. No one knew I was there and I thought I would get ate by wolves or coyotes. Finally, when my horse came back home without me, they went out looking for me.

They had a hard time finding me, but luckily I had a bright yellow rain coat on. I kept throwing my coat in the air and I was so thankful when they saw me.

My injured right leg kept me from playing football in high school, and my leg was always messed up after that.

I also remember the very first phone call I ever got. I was riding my bicycle, and I had my sister Claudia riding on the handlebars. We were peddling in front of our house, when someone yelled, "Johnny, you've got a phone call!"

I jumped off the bike with it still going. With Claudia still trying to hold on, the bike went through a ditch and hit a tree. She ended up with a broken collar bone.

When I came back out, my sister was still lying there in the ditch. She said, "What happened?"

I said, "I got a phone call."

One day, my mother went to the store with my stepfather Jim. I stayed home with Janice and Janet. They were about four or five years old, and I came up with the idea to teach them how to "flip the bird". I didn't tell them what it meant, however. Instead, I said, "When you hold up your middle finger to someone, that means, 'I love you'."

When mom and Jim pulled up in the driveway, here went these two little girls running out to meet them, and they had both of their middle fingers held proudly up in the air!

I got a good whipping for that. I had to cut my own switch off the tree. But I thought it was funny.

My family was kind of like a redneck version of the Brady Bunch... if Mrs. Brady had kept changing husbands! But even though my brothers and sisters had different fathers, all six of us kids are very close. As we were growing up, we really weren't that close, mainly because there was such a big difference in all of our ages, but we all became very close when we grew up.

Jan and I were hardly ever together when we were younger, but now, we are together all the time. She lives with me, she sells my merchandise on the road, and she runs my internet social media. And we hardly ever have a cross word. She might flip me the bird every now and then, but I know that just means she loves me!

In 1958, when I was 12 years old, my Uncle Billy and Aunt Hazel set me up on my first date. I still remember the girl's name. Her name was Lanus Turner. She had red hair. And she was a foot and a half taller than me.

We went to see the movie 'South Pacific', and I was nervous as a whore in church. At the end of the date, I tried to kiss her goodnight, but she was so tall that I jumped up to kiss her and I ended up hitting her on the nose. It actually started bleeding.

I don't know where Lanus ended up, but I think about that first kiss... every time I get a nosebleed.

The first famous person that I ever met was Roy Rogers.

I actually got to shake his hand! I touched Trigger, and I shook Roy's hand. I was about to piss all over myself. Little did I know that later in life, I'd actually get to visit with Roy and Dale at their home in California.

But our first meeting came when I was in Junior High School, when I got to go to the Houston Livestock Show and Rodeo. My mom gave me $5.00 to spend, and I spent it all on rides and games within the first hour! I couldn't do anything else for the rest of the day.

One of the carnival rides I went on before my money ran out was with a girl that I had such a crush on. Her name was Sandra Skillman, and we rode the Bullet ride, where she threw up all over me. To be honest, I thought it was kind of cool.

> "Johnny was a pretty neat kid. When he was big enough to stand up, he would grab a stick, and he would sing a song called "Chew Tobacco Rag". He would sing the song as he hit that stick.
>
> Never, ever, did it dawn on me that he would grow up to be a professional singer. And of course, he was a drummer when he was starting out. When I would watch him perform, as he hit the drums, I always remembered that little boy hitting that stick as he sang.
>
> I still remember the first gift Johnny gave me after he had hit it rich. What do you think it was? A car? A house? No. He bought me a disco light! And I loved it… so much so, that I still have it today!
>
> Johnny has been a very good son. And he is a good person. And I know that Johnny is going to be the best grandpa in the world."
>
> – Virginia Callier/Johnny Lee's Mother

CHAPTER THREE

Finding Love… and the Roadrunners

My first kiss might have been with Lanus. But my first love was Janice. Janice Smith.

I met Janice at church camp. She was 10 years old, and I was 12. We got in trouble for holding hands! They didn't want that at church camp, but we went steady in Junior High.

Janice only lived 26 miles from me, but that seemed so far when we still didn't drive yet. It was also long distance to call on the phone, so we wrote letters.

I wanted to buy her a birthstone ring. My uncle Billy loaned me the money to buy it, and Janice still has that ring today.

When I recorded my first record 'My Little Angel', Janice sang backup on the song. Her friend Martha was the other background singer. We were all just teenagers at the time.

I often went on vacations with Janice's family to San Antonio and Corpus Christi, as well, but eventually her mother made us break up because she thought we were getting too serious. And she didn't want her daughter dating someone who played music in the honky tonks. She thought I would end up in prison.

But we have still stayed in touch all of these years. We have remained very close friends through the years, and through our different marriages and divorces.

It's weird, but I still remember the address and phone number that she had back when she was a teenager.

I had always promised Janice that I would write her a song. It took me more than 50 years, but I finally did it. It's called "I Wish I Could Love That Way Again", and it's on my 'You Ain't Never Been to Texas' CD.

When I had finished writing the song in 2014, I called her and told her that I had written a song about her being my first love. I told her I would email her the song. I did, and I waited and waited for her to call and tell me if she liked it or not… but she never called. I thought, "Wow, she must not have liked her song".

I was afraid to even contact her again. Three long months went by, and then she finally called back. When I answered, she said, "I thought you were going to send me my song."

I said, "I did three months ago!" But it didn't go through on her email. I made her a CD and sent it in the mail. As soon as she got it, she called and said, "Thank you for my song. I love it so much."

They say that you never forget your first love. That is totally true in my case.

> "Johnny is one of the nicest people I know. I have known him since I was 10 years old and he was 12. He always made me feel like I was the most important person in his life.
>
> I really wasn't shocked at how big of a star he became, but I was absolutely thrilled for him.
>
> He has stayed humble all of his life, even with all of the success he had, and he is never going to change. His success will never change him.
>
> In 2014, Johnny told me he was writing a song about me being his first love. That song turned out to be 'I Wish I Could Love That Way Again'. Everything in it is true. It is my song. I love it. I thought it was the coolest thing ever. I was so honored.
>
> I wish everyone had the opportunity to know Johnny like I do. Knowing him has been the highlight of my life." - Janice K. Smith

After Janice and I broke up, I fell in love with Mary Wiggins. She said she'd go steady with me, so I gave her my FFA ring, and my FFA jacket. Our love didn't last, but she kept the ring and jacket.

They used to have sock hops at Runge Park in Arcadia. The boys would sit on one side of the room, and the girls would sit on the other side. When a boy would get up enough nerve, he would walk way across the floor and ask a girl to dance.

One night, I waited and waited until I'd built up enough courage, I walked across the room and asked the girl. And she looked straight up at me and said, "No Thanks."

It seemed like it took me forever to walk back across that floor. I knew everyone was watching. I didn't even know how to dance, anyway. It was at that moment that I told myself, "I don't want to be on the dance floor. I want to be the singer up on the stage."

I started playing the drums, and then I wanted to learn the guitar. My uncle Billy, who'd helped me buy the ring for my girlfriend Janice, also helped me get my first guitar. He loaned me the money.

And I had always wanted to sing. When I was a boy, herding cattle on our farm, I would sing all the songs I had heard on the radio. I would sing as loud as I could. The cows didn't mind.

One day in high school, a classmate George Bethune told me that he and a couple of the other guys had put together a little band, but they were needing a lead singer.

I met with the other members of the group, and I told them that I wanted to audition to be their singer. They thought I was joking, and they were surprised when I started singing 'Johnny B. Goode' for them. By the time the song had ended, I had the job. They hired me right then. And 'Johnny B. Goode' was the first song I ever sang.

We called our band the Roadrunners. The Road Runner cartoon was popular in the 50s and 60s, and we thought it was a catchy name.

At the time, there was a contest for local bands, and our group wanted to be in it. But first, we needed a place for the band to rehearse. So, I asked my mom if we could use our house. She said yes. She thought I just played drums or guitar, until the night she heard us practicing. I was singing, and she walked in. She was completely shocked! She had no idea that I could even sing.

My brother Lynn was also surprised. When he saw all the instruments in our living room, he asked me, "What's going on?"

I said, "I'm going to be singing in the FFA band."

Lynn's eyes opened wide, and he asked, "Why?"

I remember my exact words to him: "Because Ricky Nelson gets all the girls."

Our band started entering talent contests, and we won every single one that we entered. We even went on to win the state FFA talent contest.

My first paying job came when we were hired to play at Linda Benthrip's birthday party. It was at Runge Park. The building is still there. I was so scared, I was actually shaking.

We played teen dances, VFW halls, parties… they would have what they call 'Battle Dances'. They'd have two or three bands at one time. And the band that kept the most people dancing got all the money at the end of the night. And we never lost that money. We always won.

We played a dance in Palacios, Texas. We had all of our band and all of our equipment in a 1956 Pontiac. I met a girl named Donna Rice. We started making out in the backseat, and one of the guys up front said, "I smell rice burnin'."

On our way home, we almost got hit by a train. It would have killed us all. So, between the burning rice and the train, it was a memorable night.

My Grandpa Wilson was one of my biggest fans. I told grandpa that I was going to interview for a gig with Don Burns. Mr. Burns was the head of a local recreation hall at the time. I told grandpa I was scared, and he said that he would go with me for moral support. He was so cool.

Grandpa sat in on the meeting, but didn't say a word. Mr. Burns told me, "I have heard your band and you are good. How much would you charge me to play the teen hop?"

I mustered up all of my courage, then pushed my chest out, and said, "Mr. Burns, I don't think we can do it for any less than $25."

Mr. Burns looked at me and replied, "I'm sorry, I can't use you."

I said, "Why?"

He just smiled, and said, "We don't pay less than $50."

Don Burns ended up being our manager, and he actually has his name on my first record. On the 45 RPM record, it even looks like he wrote our first song, but he did not actually write it. I did.

We changed the name of our group to 'Johnny Lee and The Roadrunners' when we recorded our first record. The songs 'My Little Angel' and 'Town of No Return' got some local radio play, but when we didn't get rich and famous from the record, most of the other Roadrunners eventually decided to get real jobs. They didn't think that you could make a living off of playing music.

Today, all of the Roadrunners are still alive, except for one: Bobby Holder has passed away. Bobby was our bass player. Joe Yabbara was our drummer.

George Bethune played guitar. We called him Cubby. He was an eagle scout. And we called him Cubby, because sometimes he couldn't come to rehearse with the band because he was in scout meetings!

Claude Sommerall was also in the band. He still comes to see my shows. George Bethune also still comes to see me. Two years ago, he brought me the old Shure microphone that I had used to sing on when I was with the Roadrunners, and he gave it to me. I've now got the microphone that I sang my very first song on.

I have one more school-related note to mention, before moving on...

I was never good in English class. It was one of my worst subjects in high school, maybe because my teacher was so boring. I wish that I had paid a lot more attention in English. It would have helped me in my songwriting... and in writing this book!

CHAPTER FOUR

So You Want to See the World? How about Vietnam?

After The Roadrunners broke up, and after the breakup with my girlfriend, I had no idea where I should go next, but I knew that I wanted some adventure. So, I thought I might as well join the Marines.

I went to the recruiting office, but when I got to the Marine Corps. Office, all of the Marine guys were out to lunch. When I turned around at the door, I looked across the hall and I saw a guy in a great-looking sailor's uniform. I thought, "Man, he really looks cool."

I started talking to him, and he told me about the exciting ports, and all of the pretty girls you could find there. A few minutes later, I was signed up for the Navy! Over the next couple of years, I didn't get to see many of those ports… or many of those pretty girls. But I did get to see a lot of Vietnam!

On November 1, 1963, I boarded a plane to San Diego for boot camp. I will never forget my first night of boot camp. Everyone was scared shitless. We all got in the barracks. This kid named Dennis Cole from Iowa could do the "Donald Duck" voice. When taps blew and the lights went out, Dennis, in that duck voice, would say "I miss my mama!", and that made us all laugh.

We were in boot camp on November 22 when President Kennedy was shot.

The Kennedy Assassination was shocking, but what I am about to write will also come as a major shock to many people.

I have never told anyone this before.

Everyone thinks that my marriage to Charlene Tilton was my first, but it wasn't.

I had a cousin named Kathleen. We weren't blood cousins, she was a cousin by marriage. And she was so beautiful. I always had a crush on her, as we were growing up. I loved her, and she loved me.

Just before I was sent off to Vietnam, Kathleen got pregnant. The baby wasn't mine, but when I found out that the father of the child wasn't going to marry her, I wanted to help her out in any way that I could.

I really didn't think I was going to make it back from Vietnam, so I talked to her and I said, "Why don't we get married?" I said, "If I get killed over there, you will be taken care of. You'll get a check from the government."

I talked her into it, and we were married. She came out to California with me before I went overseas.

But truthfully, our marriage only lasted about a month. When her step dad found out she was pregnant, he came gunning for me. He thought I was the one who did it. But I wasn't. I wasn't the father. But I cared that much for her, that I married her. Our marriage was soon annulled, however, and was never mentioned again… until now.

A year after signing up for the Navy, I was sent to Vietnam, where I served on the USS Chicago. It was a brand new, state of the art missile cruiser. They said I was going to be a "plank owner"; that meant that I was part of the crew that brought the ship into commission.

Our ship sat in the Gulf of Tonkin, and launched missile attacks at targets more than a hundred miles away.

When I started on the USS Chicago, I was a "BT". That stands for "boiler tender". It is the hottest, dirtiest, and worst job in the Navy.

After working down below all day, at night we'd come up to relax. We'd sit there on the ship, and watch the air ops take off. It was a fantastic sight each and every night. We would count how many left, and then count how many came back. Sometimes they would all come back, and sometimes they wouldn't. Before I went to sleep, I always said a prayer for those who didn't come back.

One day, we were near the USS Enterprise, when it had a big phosphorous fire. A phosphorous fire is one of the hottest fires there is, and it is a miracle that ship didn't blow up. They were throwing bombs off the ship, and getting the jets off as fast as they could. They had

500,000 pounds of bombs on there. One guy was blown off the ship. We looked for two days, but never found him. We weren't able to get too close, because we had warheads aboard our vessel.

I hated being in the military. Things have changed today, and they treat everyone better. But back then, they treated the non-com like scum. Our leaders were total assholes. They could get away with anything.

The very worst so-called leader that we had was named Gretta. Gretta was a dick. There was no reason for him to be such an asshole, but he was. He would always give us extra duty. He was mean for no reason, he was a jerk, and he made it miserable for everybody. One time he cancelled everyone's liberty, just to show that he had the power to do it.

But Gretta got his payback. I am not saying who did what I am about to tell you, but somebody took a shit in a dustpan and emptied it into his bunk. Then, they took a sack of flour and covered the crap up in the flour so that he wouldn't see it. Then, someone (I'm not saying who it was, but it might have been me), took a piss all over Gretta's pillow!

When Gretta came in off of liberty, he was drunk. I happened to be in a bunk a couple aisles over. When he crawled into his bed, he slid right into that shit at the same time that he laid his head back onto that piss-soaked pillow! He started moaning, and then he started cussing, and then he jumped up and stared at his bunk. I had my face buried in my pillow! I almost had to suffocate myself to keep from laughing!

Gretta was a psycho. And speaking of psycho…

One time, I came home on leave. I told all of my younger brothers and sisters that I wanted to take them to the movies. It had not been easy on them to watch me go away to Vietnam. They had missed me, and I had missed them. But I didn't realize that the other kids might have been too young for the movie I chose. It was Alfred Hitchcock's "Psycho", and the famous shower/knife murder scene absolutely petrified my sister Jan. It scared her to death! She never took a shower again until she was in her 40s!

My family also found out that not all of the psychos were in the movies.

A man once broke into my grandma's house in Galveston, Texas. He knocked my grandma out. Me and my brother Lynn chased the guy. We finally caught him on the beach, and beat the hell out of him. We kept beating him until the police came. You have never seen a crook so relieved to see the cops coming! He almost jumped into their handcuffs.

Later, that same guy came after my twin sisters. The police had to keep them in a safehouse. The man eventually committed suicide.

During my days in the Navy, I would get so homesick. Everyone would. We always looked forward to getting mail from our family and friends. Sometimes people would send us cookies in the mail, but every time that we got them, they would all be crushed. We would take the crumbs, however, and eat 'em regardless. We were so thankful to get something like that from home.

There was one petty officer in the Navy who was OK. I want to thank Chuck Mitchell for his support and friendship. We remain friends to this day.

There was also a Mexican in my outfit. He was the biggest Mexican that I had ever seen. We called him "the Duke". His sister sent him a half gallon of jalapeno peppers in the mail one day. And these were real Mexican jalapeno peppers. I went with Duke and his friends. We ate all of those peppers, and I paid the price for the next week! I had never eaten hot food like that before. I had no idea that jalapenos were hotter when they come out of you than when they go in. They tore me up.

While we're on the subject of food: I always tell people that I once saved 516 men in my company. I shot the cook. (You have to be in the military to get that.)

I couldn't wait to get home from Vietnam, but there was one bright spot during my time in the Navy: during my free time, I was able to put a band together. We'd gather some musicians and play on the ship. We'd entertain the troops. I played the drums, and I sat right in front of a loaded guided missile. I'm glad it didn't go off.

As I was winding down my time in the Navy, my brother Lynn was just starting his service. And as soon as he finished boot camp, they put him on the same ship that I had been on.

I was thrilled to be able to spend a little time with my brother, but during the time I was stationed in California, I was less than thrilled when I ran into another, not-so familiar family member.

As luck would have it, California was where my dad had run off to, to keep from paying child support. As you'll remember, good ole dad had skipped out on my mom before I was born. My mom never talked about my dad. We never had any conversations about him. Not only did I never know the man, but I never even met my dad. I did see him once, from a distance, when he and my mom were in court for something. He wouldn't even speak to me then.

But even after all of that, here I was, 20 years old, and wanting to give my dad one last chance to be a man… and to be a father.

He came to see me a few times, and I tried to be cordial. He had remarried to another woman. She was younger than him. She was pretty attractive, and she liked to flirt with me. That was awkward. I was trying to have a relationship with my dad, and I knew that that wouldn't happen if I started fooling around with his wife.

I probably would have done her, but she had big ankles. I don't like big ankles.

But in the end, maybe I should have taken her up on the offer. Things just didn't work out with my dad and me. By then, it was a grown man coming into another grown man's life. He might have wanted to be best friends and a dad now, but it just didn't work for me. There was too much water under the bridge.

But my dad, Thomas Hamm, did leave me with one thing: the great last name of Hamm. I say 'great' sarcastically. I always hated my name. If I had known my dad, it might have been a different story.

As I was growing up, the other kids used to make fun of my name. They would yell, "Hey, Hamm Bone!" They'd insult me. It hurt my feelings. But instead of running off crying, I'd just hit them. I learned to fight at an early age.

Right after I came back from Vietnam, I asked mom what she thought about me going to court to remove my dad's name. Mom said, "That will make you no less my son. If that's what you want to do, do it."

So I had my name changed. It is legally Johnny Lee. And it upset my dad. Of course, I couldn't have cared less if he got upset!

In February 1981, I did an interview with US magazine, and they asked me about my father. I told them how he had abandoned me and my mom. Every word was true.

How did Thomas Hamm respond? He sued me! My good ole daddy said that the story had caused him to have a heart attack, and he filed a $2 million libel suit against me for "trying to ruin his good name and reputation"! What a joke! You can't make this stuff up. His lawsuit never made it to court; he never got a dime.

When he was dying, a nurse at the hospital called me. I said, "I don't even know this man. He was never there for me. He is a stranger."

I never went to his funeral.

I vowed to myself that if I was ever fortunate enough to have kids, that I would never be what he was. I wanted to be a good dad.

CHAPTER FIVE

Meeting Mickey

People ask me what I would want to do if I wasn't an entertainer, and the only other thing that I've ever wanted to be was a policeman.

After I left the military, I was going to be a highway patrolman. Law enforcement has always intrigued me. So I took the test to be a cop. I passed, but I changed my mind at the last minute. After my time in the Navy, I really just didn't want to go back to having to wear any type of uniform every day.

Today, some of my best friends are cops, highway patrolmen, and Texas Rangers. But of course, I'm too old to be a policeman now.

When I got out of the Navy, I stayed out in California for a while, where I did just about anything I could to make some money. I hired on with a highway construction crew. I helped build bridges. I was a flag man.

But I missed my family in Texas, so I eventually threw my stuff into the back of my old Chevy, and took off for the Lone Star State. My mom was living in Galveston, so that's where I was headed.

Once I got to Galveston, I got a job as a longshoreman. I worked on a dredge boat, in the boiler room. I ended up on the same pier with the same cargo that blew up back in 1947. I was a little apprehensive about it, but I needed the work.

And it was some hard-ass work. I unloaded freight and cargo all day. On my breaks, I could see all those beautiful women in bathing suits on the coast of Galveston. They were out there on the beach, and there I was in that hot dredge boat. I finally said, "This ain't for me." When the Captain's boat came out to switch Captains, I got on that boat too. I told them that they could keep my pay, I was done.

I then took a job at Montgomery Ward selling washer and dryers. I also sold car parts there. And while I was there, I started playing music at the Ceder Oaks after-hours club, too.

After we had played long into the wee hours of the morning, I was always late for my shift at Montgomery Ward. So, they gave me the choice of playing my music or pursuing my career with Montgomery Ward. I clocked out, and never went back.

My Uncle Jimmy was one of my biggest supporters. He was in the construction business, and he gave me one of my first jobs. I was his very cheap labor. He put me to work cleaning everything up, and I also helped smooth out the cement on floors so they could put down carpet. I also ran a concrete cutter on some construction sites.

Uncle Jimmy always believed in me. He was quite proud of me. He would always take me around to different clubs and talk the owners into letting me sing.

But he didn't live to see my career.

He was driving his car when someone hit him and drove off. He chased them down, and when they stopped at a light, he got out. And when he leaned down into their window, they unloaded a 9 millimeter into his face. They served less than 10 years in prison for his murder.

Before I go on stage every night, I say a prayer. And every now and then, even now, I will dedicate my show to Uncle Jimmy.

The first country song I ever sang was 'Statue of a Fool'. It was one of Jack Greene's signature songs.

To show you how crazy life is sometimes... Jack Greene's song was the first country song that I ever did. And then, years later, I sang on Jack Greene's last album that he recorded just before he died. I went to Jack's house, and did a duet with him on the Willie Nelson song 'Night Life'.

Never in my wildest dreams did I ever dream that I would become friends with Jack Greene. And to think that I would be singing with him at his house... unbelievable.

The first country star that I ever met was Skeeter Davis. I had just gotten out of the military. My uncle, Jimmy Wilson, was involved with the Starlite Ballroom in Galveston, Texas, where he promoted shows. One night, I was asked to be the drummer for Skeeter Davis. Her huge hit "The End of the World" had come out in 1962, and she also had another hit at the time called 'Something Precious".

When I found out I was going to be onstage with Skeeter, I just about crapped my pants. I was so nervous! I couldn't believe that I was playing drums and singing backup for her.

Before I had any records of my own, I only sang cover songs. I would sing Conway Twitty, Fats Domino, Ricky Nelson, whoever it was that had a hit at the time. And I would always try to sound just like them. But when I started recording, I had to try to find what *Johnny Lee* really sounded like.

I was just a small town country singer at the time. When the big country stars would come to town, I would look at their bus and dream of the day when I could get my own bus. I just wanted to be able to go on the road.

When Faron Young came in for a concert, I got to go on his bus. I couldn't believe I was in the presence of this huge star. I had no idea that, years later, I would end up becoming friends with Faron.

I got to play golf with him. He was one of the funniest guys I met in my life. I loved him. When he died, I was heartbroken. I still love him. And even to this day, I still put him in my prayers.

In 1969, I was playing drums and singing for a trio in a little club in Southeast Texas. While I was working for very little money, the man who was really hot in the area was Mickey Gilley.

Mickey was raised in Ferriday, Louisiana. He grew up with two cousins, who also became well-known. One was Jimmy Swaggart, who went into the ministry and eventually became a famous televangelist. Mickey's other cousin was Jerry Lee Lewis. When Jerry Lee rose to stardom in 1958, Mickey said, "If Jerry can do it, so can I." Like Jerry, Mickey was also a showman like no other when he sat down at the piano.

Mickey was playing shows at a place in Pasadena, Texas called the Nesadel Club. I heard that Mickey liked to play pool in between his sets. He would bet on his pool games, and most nights he was able to make more money on the pool table than he did on the stage.

I went to his show with the goal of auditioning for Mickey. I wanted him to hear me sing.

But when I got ready to introduce myself to him, I thought, "If I ask him if I can sing with him, he'll probably say no". So I walked up to him when he was playing pool. I said, "Mickey, I know you don't remember me, but I did a show with you in Galveston. I was on before you, and we had to go on to another show before you came out. So I didn't get to say hi." I was blowing smoke. I was making it all up. But I never asked to sing with him.

All of a sudden, Mickey said, "Do you want to sing a song tonight?"

I kept playing it cool as I answered, "Oh, I guess I could." I ended up singing a few songs that night. We got to know each other over the next few months, and he saw what I could do. And then, Mickey offered me a job. His offer was $90 a week…cash money! I said, "Hell yeah!" All I had to do was work six hours a night, six nights a week!

After I had worked with Mickey for a while, I asked him, "Mickey, do you remember when we first met?"

He said he did. I confessed, "I had never seen you before in my life. We hadn't worked a show together like I told you."

He said, "I kept trying to place you. But I just couldn't remember you! But I didn't want to be rude."

When I was 21, Mickey named me as his band leader. I was honored to do the job, but it was a very stressful position. It looked fun and glamorous, but it was stressful.

One night, I was playing on stage when I got sick and had to stop. After a minute or so, I picked my trumpet back up. When I started to blow into it, a bunch of blood came flying out of my mouth. I ran to the bathroom, and I started throwing up blood. After a few minutes more, I went back out on stage. I was able to play a little bit, but then I had to go throw up again. I managed to drive myself home, but when I got there, I kept throwing up blood.

After the show that night, my bass player Larry Land decided to come by to check on me. When he got there, I was passed out on the floor. I had lost so much blood. He picked me up and took me to the hospital, but since I was a country singer who didn't have any insurance, the hospital wouldn't take me in. Larry decided to take me to the VA hospital.

When we got there, they wanted to interview me and ask me all kinds of questions. But when I threw up blood all over their floor, they finally took me back to the emergency room. They ran a tube down my nose, all the way into my stomach, and they found out that I had a bleeding ulcer.

Larry Land truly saved my life that night. I would have died on my bathroom floor if he hadn't come by to check on me.

While I was recovering, there was no way that I could perform. The owners of the Nesadel said they would not pay me while I was in the hospital. Of course, I was making the huge sum of $90 a week. Mickey Gilley went to them, and told them that if they didn't pay me, he would quit. Mickey stood up for me. And I never forgot that.

Mickey also gave me my first diet pill. A lot of your favorite country stars of the 1960s and 70s took diet pills. They were really speed, an amphetamine. Some called them 'Uppers', or 'Pep Pills'. A few called them 'Pocket Rockets'. Mickey liked to date girls who were a little overweight so that he could get their diet pills. He had collected a bunch of pills. I was really tired one night, and I asked Mickey if he had anything to pep me up a little. Without saying a word, he threw six of those diet pills onto the bed. I took my hand like I was playing Jacks and scooped up all of them. I threw them into my mouth and washed them down with a swig of beer. Mickey yelled, "My God, Johnny! You were only supposed to take one!"

That night, I did the show and then drove all the way to San Antonio (a three hour trip) just to get a cup of coffee! I was keyed up.

While we were playing at the Nesadel, a man by the name of Sherwood Cryer was running a club across town called "Shelley's", which was an old barn-style building that Sherwood had turned into a nightclub. It was basically just a small bar. Sherwood had bought the club with the money he had made as a welder at Shell Oil. He also used the building as a warehouse. One of his many business ventures was as a vending machine company, so he filled the club up with jukeboxes, video games, and pool tables.

In 1971, Sherwood asked Mickey Gilley to come work for him. He told Mickey he would change the name of the club to "Gilley's", and he also promised Mickey 50% of the profits. He also said that he would expand the club so that it could hold 300 people.

Of course, the chance to see his name up in huge lights was too tempting for Mickey to pass up. Mickey and I moved from the Nesadel to the soon-to-be Gilley's.

Little did we know, we were about to change that little bar into the World's Biggest Honky Tonk!

CHAPTER SIX

Gilley's

From the time that the "Gilley's" name was put on the club, people always thought that Mickey owned and ran everything.

But it was really Sherwood Cryer who was calling every shot. The club was Sherwood's idea, Sherwood was the one who put up the money to open the business, and it was his decision to join up with Mickey that led to the club's success. Yes, Sherwood was the man in charge, but when it came to fame and fortune, Sherwood was only interested in the fortune. He had no interest in being famous. He could not have cared less whether or not anyone knew his name.

You could usually find Sherwood wearing an old zip-up coverall jumpsuit. He looked like the club janitor! No one would have believed it if you told them this guy was actually the man who owned Gilley's, and this multi-million dollar company!

Sherwood's dream of squeezing 300 people into Gilley's would explode over the next few years. We would soon expand the place so that we could hold more than 7,500 people! And later, they'd build an indoor rodeo arena that would seat another 10,000!

Sherwood never smoked, and never drank, but he made millions from those who did. He also made millions from Mickey Gilley and Johnny Lee. But you wouldn't have thought that, by the way he treated us.

One small example...we would be singing at Gilley's until 2:00 am. When the time changed from Daylight Savings time each year, and we had to turn our clocks back one hour, Sherwood would always screw us.

When the clocks were supposed to go forward one hour, he would wait until 2:00 am to change them.

But when the clocks went back an hour, he would change them at midnight, so we would have to work an extra hour for free.

To help save on expenses, for almost nine years I lived with an oil-working friend named Robert Small. He and I shared a house that was near Gilley's.

But Mickey was excited to see his name up in lights on the Gilley's club. And I also got my first taste of fame when we started producing a local TV show called "Gilley's Place". Even though my name wasn't in the title, it really showcased both of us. Mickey would do his songs, and I would do mine, and then we'd always have a special guest on.

A furniture store sponsored the show. "Gilley's Place" aired on Channel 39. And the TV show was the thing that really helped the Gilley's club start to grow in popularity. Everyone who watched the show wanted to come and see us in person.

Every night at Gilley's was like New Year's Eve to me. But on the real New Year's Eve, we would dress up a little nicer. Me and Gilley and the band would come up in the day, and we would spend the entire day decorating the place. We'd put different cash prizes in balloons, and then we'd tie the balloons up in the ceiling. We did it all.

While I enjoyed my local fame from the "Gilley's Place" TV show, Mickey was beginning to find nationwide stardom. Hugh Hefner, the founder of Playboy Magazine, wanted to help his girlfriend Barbi Benton get into country music. She was already on the TV show 'Hee Haw', so Hugh started 'Playboy Records'. Barbi recorded some songs for the label, but they also signed Mickey Gilley.

And, in 1974 and '75, Mickey had four straight number 1 songs! Three of them were "Room Full of Roses", "I Overlooked an Orchid", and "Bouquet of Roses". I told Mickey, "You ought to open a flower shop!"

In 1975, Mickey also had a huge hit with "Don't the Girls All Get Prettier at Closing Time". Mickey originally thought the song would offend women. But his worries evaporated, as he watched the song skyrocket to the top of the charts. It was a song that all of the cowboys who came to Gilley's could relate to. And all of the women said, "Hey, the guys also get better looking as the night goes on!"

When he became one of the hottest guys in country music, Mickey had to start touring on the road. He had to cut back on his time at the club that had his name. And to make up for Mickey's absence, I increased my time on stage.

Each day, I would rehearse at Gilley's during the day, and then play for six hours each night. The most I ever made during that time was $500 a week, working five nights a week. I did that for eight years!

In addition to the guitar, I also played the trumpet, and a little bit of banjo. When 'The Cotton Eyed Joe' came out, I thought it was so cool, so I went out and bought me a fiddle. I sat in front of my record player and played 'The Cotton Eyed Joe', and I taught myself to play it. I practiced all day.

When I thought that I had learned just enough, I took my fiddle to Gilley's. I thought I would surprise the band. But when I started playing it with them, they were just a little bit out of tune with my fiddle. I only knew it one way. So after that, they would hide my fiddle bow whenever they could.

While I enjoyed singing in the club, and I was able to make a living (barely), I really had a feeling that something big was going to happen in my career. I was thrilled with the success of my buddy Mickey. To be honest, I might have been a little jealous at times… but I was also very inspired by him. I knew, if he had made it big, then I could too.

One night, my band backed up Michael Martin Murphy, and after the show he stayed at my house. We stayed up all night, playing guitars and singing. He said, "I've got a song you might want to record," and he sang "Cherokee Fiddle". He ended up singing harmony when I eventually recorded it. Charlie Daniels played the fiddle on the record. And Rosemary Butler also sang on it. She was known for her work with Jackson Browne and Linda Rondstadt.

In the summer of 1978, a writer from Esquire Magazine paid a visit to Gilley's. He was so intrigued with the club that he wrote a long feature story about it. It was titled, "The Ballad of the Urban Cowboy".

The story focused on the hardworking, blue collar type of folks from Southeast Texas "who liked to play as hard as they worked". And they worked hard. Each Friday and Saturday night. We were playing to 4,000 oil refinery workers, truck drivers and ranchers.

In 1978, those who visited Gilley's came for the live country music and the beer. Of course, each single man was looking for a girl, and each girl was looking for a cowboy. Gilley's also offered 50 pool tables, punching bag machines, and a thing called a mechanical bull. The bull gave the cowboys a nice chance to show off for their potential cowgirl.

Mickey told Sherwood he shouldn't have the mechanical bull, because people would sue us if they got thrown off and broke their neck. So Sherwood put up a sign that said, "Ride at your own risk". That sign seemed to actually make more people want to try riding the bull. We watched from the stage as one person after another got thrown off like a rag doll onto a big pile of mattresses.

Speaking of the mattresses… Sherwood would also drive around Pasadena, looking for old mattresses that people had put out at their trash. He would take all those old mattresses and put them under the mechanical bull for people to fall on. He wasn't about to buy any new mattress! If you landed on one of those old mattresses and didn't leave with something on you, you were very fortunate.

The Esquire story also showcased a couple, Dew and Betty, who had met at Gilley's. They first met when they were 18 years old, and had gotten married a year later. They were known for riding the mechanical bull. Betty could ride the bull standing up, and she could do all kinds of other tricks on it.

The feature story caught the attention of someone with the Jerry Lewis Labor Day Telethon, and the first national exposure I ever got was when I appeared on the Telethon in 1978.

Mickey and I were both on the show. This was before I had had any hits, so I sang 'Hey Good Lookin' and 'If You've Got the Money, I've Got the Time'. You can find this entire thing on YouTube, and it really is a classic!

You'll see that the huge orchestra wouldn't start the song. I don't know why they didn't start the music, but I had to kill about two minutes. I finally went over and kissed Jerry Lewis! I don't think Jerry even knew who I was, but he saw that I was dressed up like a cowboy and he said, "Rootin', tootin', fig nootin'!"

And for some reason, the show's producers had the Oakland Raiderette cheerleaders dancing behind me! The entire group were waving their pom poms as I sang. After the show, I ended up hooking up with two of the Raiderettes. I was out at the swimming pool. And this was back when I looked good in a swimming suit! All those cheerleaders were there. It was like a buffet.

In early 1979, I started hearing rumors that someone in Hollywood had read the Esquire article, and they were hoping to turn it into a movie.

I didn't pay much attention to those rumors until that summer, when the trucks from Hollywood started rolling in.

Once we'd found out that the movie was for real, we all started wondering who was going to be starring in it. One night, in between sets, I saw a man with dark hair and a dark, heavy beard. He had his cowboy hat pulled down low. He watched the folks try to ride the mechanical bull, and he didn't say much to the other patrons.

Finally, a guy came up to me and said, "Do you know who that is?"

I looked at him and said, "Nope, who?"

They said, "That's John Travolta!"

I looked closer at the guy with the beard. I smiled, and whispered, "It sure as hell is." John Travolta was one of the biggest stars going. He had starred in the blockbusters Grease and Saturday Night Fever, and now he was holding a beer as he listened to the music at Gilley's!

I didn't say anything to John that night. I just let him hang out and soak in the atmosphere. But a few days later, I met him for the very first time. He was kind of shy, but very nice.

When I found out that he was the star of this movie, I knew this was not some small production. This was the big time!

Once word got out that they were filming 'Urban Cowboy' at Gilley's, people packed the place. The club was already very popular, but this was something totally different. Every day and every night, the Spencer Highway that leads to Gilley's was bumper to bumper.

People from all over wanted to try and catch a glimpse of the movie stars. They also wanted to see what was so special about this place that would make Hollywood want to turn it into a major motion picture.

What is the one word that I would use to describe the filming at Gilley's? HOT. Remember, all of the filming took place in the middle of summer in Texas. And while the club was air conditioned, the cooling system was too loud when they were shooting, so it had to be turned off. That building got hot and humid almost instantly.

The movie makeup people had one of the toughest jobs. They would put everyone's makeup on, and by the time they started filming the scene, we would be so wet with sweat that the makeup was gone. But, that helped with the club's beer sales. "Cold beer! Get your cold beer!"

While I was thrilled that John Travolta was in the film, I was even more impressed with his co-star. When she walked into the club, Debra Winger looked like a living angel.

Debra was not only very cute, but she was also real down to earth and very friendly. Shortly after we met, I gave her a Lone Star armadillo pin for her hat. And she wore that pin throughout the movie. I also gave her lessons on how to say the word "bull". Both Debra and John were trying to sound as authentic as they could, but for some reason they had trouble mastering some words in that Texas accent. As I taught Debra how to say "bull", she also used the same technique when she said the name "Bud". And she had to say "Bud" about a hundred times in the movie! I had a major crush on Debra, and I went out with her a time or two after the movie was filmed.

John Travolta played the role of Bud, and Debra played the role of Sissy. In real life, Bud and Sissy were really Dew and Betty, the couple who had met at Gilley's, and who were originally written about in the Esquire story. Dew and Betty ended up getting divorced, but I still see each of them every now and then when I play in Texas.

The movie's cast also included Scott Glenn, who played Wes, the bad guy. In real life, Scott Glenn is one of the nicest gentlemen you will ever meet. Barry Corbin played Bud's Uncle Bob. Barry still comes to see me. He is still a fan of mine. And Madolyn Smith played Pam. Madolyn was stunningly beautiful. She was even more beautiful in person than she was on screen.

The first time that I ever rode the mechanical bull, the folks from Paramount Pictures were there. They told me to get on and show them how it worked, but I had never been on it. I sat up about six inches from the rigging, and when they cranked that thing up, I thought I would never be able to become a father.

But I eventually got good at riding the bull. I could ride it when it was wide open.

I enjoyed being a part of the filming of the movie, but I was still only planning to be an extra, playing in the band behind Mickey Gilley. But those plans changed one night, when a short little Jewish guy heard me singing 'Cherokee Fiddle'. After I had finished my set, I headed to the bar (as always) when a man stopped me and said, "My name is Irving Azoff. You wanna be in the movie?"

I said, "I damn sure do".

Irving smiled and said, "OK. I'm going to make a star out of you, boy."

I had no idea who Irving Azoff was. After he walked away, I said to my buddies, "Yeah right. You're gonna make me a star."

Someone said, "Man, do you know that guy?! He manages the Eagles, Journey and Fleetwood Mac!" It was at the precise moment that I knew that Johnny Lee's ship was about to come in! Or at least I was hoping it was.

Mr. Azoff told me that he wanted to include the song 'Cherokee Fiddle' in the movie, and he also wanted me to look for one or two more songs that I could sing. He asked me to meet with the movie's music coordinator, Becky Shargo, at a hotel in Houston.

When Becky and I walked into the hotel room, it was filled with cardboard boxes, and each box was filled with cassette tapes. We started digging through the tapes, as we listened to a few seconds of each song. Within the first dozen songs that I had listened to, I found one marked 'Lookin' for Love'. When I played it, I said, "My God, I can't believe I didn't write that myself!"

I'll talk much more about 'Lookin' for Love', but right now we have a major motion picture world premiere to go to!

CHAPTER SEVEN

Urban Cowboy

On June 5, 1980, the world premiere for 'Urban Cowboy' was held at a theater in Houston, Texas.

I rented a limousine to take me to the premiere. I really couldn't afford it, but by God, I did it. When Gilley found out that I had rented the limo, he gave me some shit. Then I looked at how he came to the movie. He was in his pickup truck! I said, "You redneck."

My date that night was a beautiful woman whom I was hoping to get to know much better after the movie.

As I sat there watching the movie, I started out thinking, "This is great. I am going to get lucky with this girl tonight!" But by the time the movie was over, I had completely forgotten about the girl. I knew that my life was going to be changed forever!

All throughout the movie, they kept playing MY song! 'Lookin' for Love' was in the first part of the film. And then they kept playing it, over and over. And they even put an orchestrated version of 'Lookin for Love' at the end of the movie. But the best part was in the scene where it is playing on the radio, and John Travolta says "Hey, turn that up, that's my favorite song." It freaked me out!

The Urban Cowboy soundtrack included a who's who of musical superstars.

Kenny Rogers had a song in the movie. Boz Scaggs, Linda Ronstadt, Anne Murray, Bonnie Raitt, Jimmy Buffett, Bob Segar, the Eagles, Dan Fogleberg and Joe Walsh all had songs in it. The Charlie Daniels Band sang the song that became his biggest hit ever, 'The Devil Went Down To Georgia', and of course, Mickey Gilley had a number of songs in the movie.

I thought that 'Stand By Me' was going to be the big song in the film. It was Gilley's club. It was Gilley's name throughout the movie. And I was always sucking hind tit behind Mickey, so I figured he would have the biggest hit.

But as soon as Mickey saw the movie, he told everyone, "Johnny Lee has got a hit!" And Mickey was right.

There were huge hit songs that came out of 'Urban Cowboy', but it was MY song that came to the very top. How crazy is that? It is a blessing. I was flabbergasted. I was 33 years old when I had my first hit song! Today's country artists are considered too old if they don't have a hit by the time they are 24.

People think that I got rich from being in 'Urban Cowboy'. John Travolta might have gotten rich, but Johnny Lee didn't. I got paid scale to be in the movie. 'Scale' is basically the minimum wage for movies.

But that was alright by me, because when 'Urban Cowboy' came out, it was like I was loaded into the world's biggest slingshot and thrown into the stars! I had waited my entire life for this moment. I would try my best to keep up with everything, but it turned out to be wilder and crazier than anything I could have imagined.

As soon as 'Urban Cowboy' was shown across the country, sales of western clothing exploded. The Tony Lama boot company had to build two new factories, just to keep up with the demand for cowboy boots. And it seemed like everyone was wearing a cowboy hat like mine. I am the one who really got the Charlie 1 Horse hats going. I was the first famous person to wear one.

Sherwood Cryer started selling his El-Toro mechanical bulls for $8,500 to bars and carnivals across the country.   He had to hire more than 30 people to build the bulls, and even then, he had a two-month waiting list.

Cryer was also selling anything that you could write "Gilley's" on. That included everything from T-shirts and jeans, to belt buckles and ashtrays, and even ladies' panties! But the one thing that was outselling everything else was my song 'Lookin' for Love'!

The 'Lookin' for Love' single was released to radio in June of 1980, and on August 31, it hit #1 on the Billboard Hot Country Singles Chart. It would stay at the top of the charts for the next three weeks. By the way, the B-Side of the 45 record was the song 'Lyin' Eyes' by the Eagles!

'Lookin' for Love' was the story of my life, and I couldn't believe it when I found out who wrote the song. It was written by two school teachers in Mississippi! Wanda Mallette of Gulfport and Patti Ryan of Long Beach had never had a song recorded by anyone. They also had some help from Bob Morrison from Nashville. They all ended up making more money from that song than I did.

The two teachers got the idea for the song from a classroom of second graders. They said they noticed that the children who had always seemed to get in trouble were the ones who had the worst home life. And Wanda Mallette said, "Those kids are just looking for love in all the wrong places."

A few years ago, I was playing at a casino in Gulf Port. I was signing autographs after the show, and there was this group of people in line. The group was that very same second grade class of kids that 'Lookin' for Love' came from. They were all grown up now!

Wanda and Patti went on to write another number one song. In 1984, Anne Murray took their 'Just Another Woman in Love' to the top of the charts, and Patti also wrote 'Americana' for Moe Bandy.

After I found the cassette tape of the song they had sent in, I changed the arrangement and rhythm and made it a two-step. We went into the studio in Los Angeles to record the song, but they somehow lost the original recording. I don't know exactly what happened. I don't know if it got erased, or what, but I had to go back in and re-record it. Luckily, I still had a work tape from the first one.

John Boylan, who was Linda Ronstadt's producer, was sitting behind the control board. He produced 'Lookin' for Love' and 'Cherokee Fiddle'. They were the two most memorable songs of my career. But Jim Ed Norman eventually came in and produced the rest of the 'Lookin' for Love' album, and I never worked with John Boylan again. I never could figure out why. When your producer owns the publishing on certain songs, those are always the ones they want to release as singles. That helps the producer, but it's not always good for the artist.

I started singing 'Lookin' for Love' at Gilley's just before 'Urban Cowboy' came out, and people would dance as I sang. But after the movie was released, everyone stopped dancing. Instead, they just stood and watched me sing it. That is very rare at a dance club in Texas. I knew it was something very special.

'Lookin' for Love' is a song that will outlive me. Kids who were not even thought of back then now know the words to 'Lookin' for Love'.

I have heard so many stories about that song. People have said, "That song is what got me into country music,"̦ "I met my wife to that song,"̦ "That song was played at our wedding,"̦ and "That song was played at my dad's funeral."

So how do you follow up a career song like 'Lookin' for Love'? Everyone was waiting to see what kind of song we would come out with next. And I knew that I had another big hit just waiting. We had already recorded it, and it was on the same album.

I wanted my record company to release my song called 'Do You Love As Good As You Look'. I thought that it just made sense, especially with 'Look' and 'Love' in the title!

But my producer, Jim Ed Norman, didn't have the publishing rights to that song. And I was about to get my first lesson in song publishing in Nashville.

Jim Ed did have the publishing on a tune called "One in a Million", so he chose to release it. I was disappointed, but I felt better as I watched "One in a Million" go to number one. But, only a short time later, I heard the Bellamy Brothers' new song on the radio. It was 'Do You Love As Good As You Look'. It was not only a big number 1 for them, but it also became a huge crossover hit for the Bellamys!

While I kept having new hits, for the next year or so, 'Lookin' for Love' won award after award.

In 1980, I won the Academy of Country Music Top New Male Vocalist Award. That year, the Urban Cowboy soundtrack also won the ACM for Album of the Year.

I was presented with my first gold record for my album 'Lookin' for Love'. My friend Steve Howe, from the Los Angeles Dodgers, came to Gilley's to give me the award.

But I didn't win every single award that I was nominated for. I went to the Grammy Awards when 'Lookin' for Love' was up for a

Grammy. I stood backstage with George Jones when George won the Grammy for his song 'He Stopped Loving Her Today'. I really didn't mind because the entire time I was thinking, "Hell, I'm standing here beside the great George Jones!" Of course now, many people say that that song is the greatest country song of all time, so I shouldn't have been too upset.

Another disappointment came in 1981, when I was nominated at the Music City News awards for Most Promising New Male Artist. Since I was on such a roll, I had no doubt that I would win. But I got quite a shock when they read, "And the winner is... Boxcar Willie!"

I was happy for him, but I was in shock. Boxcar was 50 years old! And he beat me for Most Promising NEW Artist?! I knew that Boxcar had been singing his songs since I was three years old. I couldn't believe it. But I really did like Boxcar a lot and he was a tremendous entertainer.

But some things are bigger than any award, and I was about to find out exactly how huge my 'Lookin' for Love' song really was.

October 10, 1981. 'Saturday Night Live', Episode 2 of Season 7.

The popular TV show 'Saturday Night Live' was broadcast each week, live from New York City. As luck would have it, I happened to be in New York with the Marshall Tucker Band and Rosanne Cash that weekend. And I started hearing people saying something about the TV show 'Saturday Night Live'.

Comedian Eddie Murphy had done a skit in which his character Buckwheat sang his 'greatest hits'. And one of those hits was Buckwheat's version of 'Lookin' for Love' - 'Wookin' Pa Nub'. The next day, it seemed that everyone I saw was singing "Wookin' Pa Nub!"

I thought it was great. I thought it was cool. My one regret is that I wasn't at the show in person when they did it. If I had known that they were doing it, I would have loved to have just shown up to be on 'Saturday Night Live'.

In 2014, 'Rolling Stone' magazine ranked the 'Buckwheat Sings' spot as the second-greatest Saturday Night Live sketch of all time!

And I still love it. I was going to put WKN PU NUB on my license plate, but it was one letter too many. I have still never met Eddie Murphy, but when I do, I'm going to give him a hug and say "Thank you". People asked me, "Didn't that make you mad?" Hell no! Are you kidding? I loved it. 'Wookin' Pa Nub'. That's O-Tay with me!

People ask me how many times I have sung 'Lookin' for Love', and I tell them, "Not enough." I never get tired of singing that song.

CHAPTER EIGHT

A Ride Wilder Than a Mechanical Bull

To say that my life had been turned upside down would be an understatement.

We sold out the Nassau coliseum in New York City. We sold out Riverfront Stadium in Cincinnati, where Pete Rose and The Cincinnati Reds played! We had 24,000 people at the Silverdome in Pontiac Michigan. We played the Chicago Pier. There were a couple hundred thousand people there to see me, and Charlie Daniels, Mickey Gilley and Alabama. Yeah, we were pretty hot.

Mickey was asked to sing the National Anthem at a Sugar Ray Leonard fight. He was afraid he would forget the words, so he recorded the song on a cassette and had planned to lip-sync to the tape. At fight time, the color guard marched in. Gilley stood there. The people around him said, "Sing!"

He whispered, "Play the tape." Nothing. He turned and said, "Play the tape!" They say, "The tape is broke". He had to sing it live. He might have re-wrote it a little, but he got through it.

I opened hundreds of shows for Mickey, but I always tell people that Mickey closed all of my shows for me. If you say it that way, I sound more impressive.

During one concert, Mickey called me out for an encore. We were doing the Charlie Daniels song, 'The South's Gonna Do It Again'. It has a lot of words, and it is fast. If you get messed up on it, you really mess up. And I totally forgot the words. I stood there, and then panic began to set in. I knew I was in trouble. We finally just turned it all over to the fiddle player.

In March of 1981, I did an interview with People Magazine, and I made a statement that I still get asked about. I told the reporter, "The more successful a guy gets, the better quality of women he gets."

That statement has followed me around ever since. My manager got so mad when I said it. Here's what I meant by that: had I not been doing what I was doing, having the hits and success that I was, I would never have met a woman like Charlene Tilton. I did not mean it as a disrespect to women at all! But it is the truth. I think that every woman wants a husband who is successful at whatever he does for a living.

I was in awe of what was happening in my life and in my career. To be honest, I was in shock. I was so thankful. I had been working my whole life for this. It was a dream come true. I am thankful and blessed to have gotten to experience that.

My biggest fear was of falling off the stage. All the lights were hitting us. All the cameras were flashing, but I couldn't even see the faces of the people in the front row. I came close to falling off a couple of times. I was trying to shake someone's hand, and they almost pulled me off the stage.

I was once invited to sing on The Grand Ole Opry. I took my mom with me. I wanted her to be a part of this huge moment for me. She was backstage before the show, and then went out front to take pictures of my Opry debut. But her camera broke, and she wasn't able to get any photos.

I did a concert in in Ireland. I was on the show along with Tammy Wynette, Jerry Lee Lewis, Bobby Bare, and the "Most Promising New Male Artist", Boxcar Willie!

The coliseum was packed. They loved us. Every place we went, they loved us.

But everywhere we went in Ireland, we were escorted by military humvees. They had machine guns in the front and in the back. It was a true warzone.

In Belfast, there were barbed wire fences around our hotel. They told us to leave our hotel room lights off, and to not walk around in our room after dark.

But I wanted to get some Irish whiskey. So I walked downtown. I was wearing my cowboy hat and boots, and as I carried two bottles of whiskey back to my hotel, everyone looked at me like I was from another planet. I think they were too busy trying to figure out what I was that they forgot to shoot me.

Every now and then, someone will jokingly say, "The world couldn't handle two Johnny Lees!"

But in 1980, for a short time, there actually were two Johnny Lees.

There was a guy in Winter Haven, Florida who was telling people that he was Johnny Lee. He was impersonating me, and he was a scam artist.

The man went so far as to do radio interviews, and during one of those, he committed to doing a benefit concert. The radio station put him up in a fancy hotel, he ran up a huge bar bill, and then he skipped out.

Then he met a girl, and told her he was me. He had her so fooled that he got "engaged" to her! It was another scam.

He finally got caught, when a radio DJ asked him which record label he was with. He said that he was on BMI, and that threw up a red flag. The station contacted the sheriff's office, and he ended up getting arrested.

I never did meet the guy, but later on, I did meet the woman he had gotten "engaged" to. And I ended up going out with her! We went to my hotel, and the next morning, she said, "Of all of the Johnny Lees in the world, I like you the best!"

We were drawing huge crowds to our road shows, and the crowds continued to pack the place when we returned home to Pasadena.

I was so popular that Sherwood Cryer bought the old Nesadel Club where he had found me and Mickey. He renamed it "Johnny Lee's Club". Since we were having to turn people away from Gilley's because it was so packed, we used "Johnny Lee's Club" as an overflow. When Gilley's sold out, the rest of the crowd went to "Johnny Lee's".

One of the most clever marketing ideas that Sherwood ever came up with was the Gilley's bumper sticker.

Back in the 70s and 80s, you would see the stickers on every other car that you would pass. The stickers were white with red letters that simply said "Gilley's Pasadena Texas".

Gilley's was the most popular bumper sticker there was. "See Ruby Falls" stickers would have come in second. They were a rolling advertisement for the club.

While most tourist destinations charge you to buy a bumper sticker as a souvenir, at Gilley's, they gave you a sticker... whether you wanted one or not! They even put it on your car... again, even if you didn't want one!

Sometimes, people would drive their expensive cars to the club and they didn't want a sticker put on their bumpers. So, Sherwood came up with an idea.

If someone didn't want a sticker, all they had to do was put their sun visor down when they parked. When Sherwood's workers (a bunch of illegal Mexicans) would walk through the parking lots with stickers, they would pass by all the cars that had the visors down.

At least, that's what Sherwood told people. But that is not what happened. Those Mexicans weren't about to take the time to see if any visors were down. It was the biggest joke in the world. If your car was in the parking lot, you were going to get a bumper sticker!

So, what difference did that make? What was the big deal? Here's what happened many times: some guy would go to Gilley's. When he got home, he told his wife he had been working and he did not go out anywhere. But the wife would walk out to the car, and it would have that big, bright white-and-red Gilley's sticker plastered on the back bumper. She knew where he had been!

And I don't know what they were made of, but you could not get them off. Even today, decades later, you can go to any junkyard in Texas and you will see old cars. They are all rusted out and don't run, but they still have that Gilley's sticker on their bumper. And that sticker looks brand new.

Whenever Mickey or I weren't headlining at Gilley's, some other big star was. Everyone who was anyone performed there. Everybody from Fats Domino to Conway Twitty and Loretta Lynn. George Jones, Faron Young and Johnny Paycheck all played Gilley's. Even Weird Al Yankovic sang there. And Tiny Tim! I said, "Tiny Tim! Are you kidding me? At Gilley's?!" Guess what? He filled Gilley's up, and he did one of the best shows I've ever seen.

Sherwood also booked David Allen Coe there, and Mickey ended up making him very mad. Mickey told Sherwood that he shouldn't book David. Mickey didn't think that his music would be good in the club, and he didn't like people who cussed on stage. But Sherwood overruled him, and he booked David. And as soon as he walked in the door, Sherwood met him and said, "David, Mickey don't want you here." David got angry, but as soon as Mickey saw him, he apologized. And David ended up bringing in one of the biggest crowds that we'd ever had. And he did one of the best shows, too.

You never knew who was going to show up at Gilley's. We had so many people who you would never expect there. Since we were in Texas, where the space program was so big, we always had famous astronauts come and see us.

Alan Shepard was the second man to walk on the moon, but I remember the day he walked into Gilley's. He introduced himself, and stuck out his hand. I pushed his hand away and said, "I don't want to shake your hand. I want to shake your foot! That's what touched the moon!" He let me shake his foot, and then I shook his hand.

Mickey Gilley, Charley Pride and I were all invited to come play for the NASA folks before one of the first space shuttle launches in Florida.

Pete Conrad came to Gilley's. Pete was the third man to walk on the moon. He was also part of NASA's Skylab missions. Pete always told me to get a haircut. It's ironic that, after all of his very dangerous space travel, Pete Conrad died in a motorcycle accident in 1999.

Ellison Onizuka was the Hawaiian astronaut who was on the space shuttle Challenger. He was also on other shuttle missions. Ellison loved my music, and he gave me a wonderful autographed photo of the shuttle lifting off. I have it hanging proudly on my wall. He also invited me to NASA headquarters, to fly in a flight simulator, but I was too booked-up with shows and I never got the chance.

Ellison had a tape of mine with him when he boarded the Challenger. My music almost made it into space, but the shuttle exploded and Ellison was killed.

Kenny Stabler was one of the greatest quarterbacks in NFL history. Kenny came to Gilley's when he was playing for the Houston Oilers. I was in awe of him. But we became great friends. We used to ride our motorcycles around town. We'd drink beer and shoot pool. Kenny liked to party. And we partied.

One day, we'd been riding our motorcycles, and I had to get to Gilley's to do my show. We decided to ride our bikes right through the front door. We rode past the pool tables and circled around the mechanical bull, driving right up to the stage. I got off, did my show, and then we hopped back on the motorcycles and rode out.

We also had a lot of major league baseball players come to the club. Hall of Fame manager Tommy Lasordo loved Gilley's. I also became friends with Rick Sutcliff, Steve Howe, and Steve Garvey. New York Yankee legend Billy Martin loved it there. He traded rings with me for one night. I gave him one of my big diamond rings, and he let me wear his World Series ring.

When 'Urban Cowboy' hit and we became the hottest acts in Country music, Mickey and I began a very heavy touring schedule. But even though we were doing huge concerts across the country, as soon as we got in from the road, we were expected to be on stage at Gilley's to earn our $500 a week.

To keep up our jet-set lifestyle, Mickey bought… a turbo jet.

I was with him when he was just starting to fly his own plane. He was still learning. He had a little two-seater Cessna. We were flying and joking around, when at one point I noticed Mickey got real quiet. He said, "Johnny, I think we are lost."

I looked at him and said, "How the hell do you get lost up in the sky?!"

But he finally got it figured out, and we reached our destination.

As he got more successful, Mickey's planes got bigger. He advanced on to a Cessna 210. It was almost like having our own airline. Then, we went together and got a King-Air.

I always trusted Mickey behind the controls, but he has actually crashed three times. Luckily, I was not with him on any of those occasions. Once, his landing gear wouldn't come down. One time, he hydroplaned off the runway. But he is still alive, so he must be a pretty good pilot.

And just when we thought that our careers couldn't get any higher, the television offers started rolling in.

On September 12, 1980, I sang 'Lookin' for Love' on NBC's 'The Midnight Special'. The next day, I sang the song on the nationally-syndicated show 'Solid Gold'.

I performed on The Mike Douglas and Merv Griffin Shows. I was on The Dukes of Hazard, and on the show "Emergency", I delivered a singing telegram to a nurse.

I did Fantasy Island with Linda Thompson. Linda had been Elvis' longtime girlfriend. She and I dated after our Fantasy Island episode, but a short time later she met Olympic gold medalist Bruce Jenner. They ended up getting married... before Bruce became a woman.

Herve Villechaize played Tattoo on Fantasy Island. Herve was the little guy who always opened the show by saying "Da Plane! Da Plane!" He was about three feet tall. But he was a big fan of mine, and came to a lot of my shows. I think he also liked the pretty women who came to my shows.

Herve liked guns, and always carried a derringer in his boot. He also had two huge bodyguards who always followed him around. One night, he was in my dressing room with his back against the door. My piano player R.P. Harrell burst through the door, and the doorknob hit Herve right in the back of the head. It just about knocked him down. He grabbed his head and yelled, "Da Pain! Da Pain!"

I appeared on 'CHIPS', and I became friends with Erik Estrada. I was also on 'The Fall Guy', which starred Lee Majors. Lee and me are still friends.

One of the more unique TV appearances I did was with Alan Thicke. Alan had a show called 'Thicke of the Night', I was booked on the show, and another guest was the World Tobacco Spitting Champion. They asked if I would have a contest against the World Champ to see who could spit the farthest. He ended up beating me by four inches.

I was on all of those TV shows, and I am thankful for all of those opportunities and for all of that national exposure. It sure did put my face in front of a lot of people, and it made me pretty popular.

But I have one big regret that still eats at me.

I should have been on the Johnny Carson and David Letterman

shows!

My management was stupid for not putting me on those shows. They put Gilley on them, but they wouldn't put me on. And I had the biggest song of the year! I had the number one country song and the number two song on the pop charts. It still pisses me off. I had such stupid management!

It wasn't Johnny Carson or David Letterman who said 'no', it was the people who were protecting Gilley. And it wasn't Mickey's fault. I'm sure he will admit that it was so stupid for them to not have me on those shows.

I was really bitter about that for a long time. But I had to let it go.

I was able to get to know a lot of Hollywood stars, but there was one very special TV star who I would soon get to know very well. Her name was Charlene.

CHAPTER NINE

Charlene

Charlene Tilton was born on December 1, 1958.

Charlene's mother was ill, and her dad had left right after she was born. She was sent to different foster homes when she was just a little girl. But she was able to overcome that very tough childhood.

When she was only 15 years old, she was living on her own in an apartment. Two years later, Charlene was cast in the role of 'Lucy' on the CBS TV show 'Dallas'. 'Dallas' became the most popular show on television, and Charlene became one of the most popular sex symbols on TV in the 1970s and 80s.

My first impression of Charlene? She was drop-dead gorgeous. And she was tiny! She only stood at 4'11" inches tall, but she took command of a room whenever she walked in!

"Even before I had met Johnny, 'Lookin' for Love' was one of my favorite songs. And I still think it is one of the greatest songs of all time.

When we were expecting our baby, I had come up with the name 'Cherish'. I was raised in foster homes, and I wanted to make sure that my daughter knew that she was more than loved, she was cherished.

And back then, you didn't know if you were having a boy or a girl until the day they were born.

When I went into labor, we were on the way to the hospital, and Johnny said, "If it is a girl, we will name her Cherish. What if we have a boy?"

I said back, "I want a strong, biblical name. I'd like something like Isaiah or Noah."

"What about Bucky?" Johnny asked.

> I said, "No son of mine is going to be named Bucky Lee! And if we have a boy, I am going to grab that birth certificate before you can get to it, Johnny! I know you will write Bucky on it!"
>
> Johnny is a great showman. He just loves being in front of an audience. As an actress, I love being on a movie set. I know that as a singer and entertainer, Johnny loves being up on a stage. And Johnny Lee is still an amazing entertainer today."
>
> – Charlene Tilton

Charlene's version of meeting me is different from my version of how we met. But this is my book.

I was on a date with Erin Moran. Erin played Joanie on 'Happy Days'. We were at Dick Clark's 25th Anniversary of American Bandstand show. I was in the all-star band, where I sang and played guitar, and Stevie Wonder played piano.

We were sitting at a table. Charlene was with her manager. He was kind of dating her. I didn't know that at the time, but I asked his permission to talk to her. And she told me that she had always wanted to meet Stevie Wonder, so I took her backstage. We met Stevie, and before we had gotten back to the table, I had Charlene's phone number.

That night after I took Erin home, I went home and I called Charlene. You know how some people say you should wait a couple days before you call a girl? I threw that right out the window. I couldn't wait to call her!

We dated less than a year before we were married.

Charlene had gotten pregnant. I had to talk to her a long time, but I finally talked her into marrying me.

We got married on Valentine's Day, 1982. Our wedding was held at Liza Minnelli's house in Lake Tahoe. Mickey Gilley was my best man. Tony Orlando was also there.

I was 35 years old when I married Charlene. She was 23.

We didn't know whether Charlene was going to have a boy or a girl. We wanted to wait until the baby was born. Charlene swears that if we had had a son, I would have wanted to name our child "Bucky".

I do not agree! I wanted to name him Jubal! Jubal Lee. I did NOT want to name our kid Bucky! I really did want Jubal. In the Bible, Jubal is the father of music. I figured that our son would either really like it, or really hate it and want to whip my ass when he grew up.

But our baby turned out to be a girl. And I thought Charlene's idea for her name was perfect: Cherish. Cherish was born on August 20, 1982. I was there when she was born. I helped with the delivery, and it was a very emotional experience for me.

The trash magazines and tabloids offered me a lot of money, and any kind of car I wanted, if I would give them pictures of our baby.

Like a fool, I didn't take them up on the offer. I should have taken the car! But Charlene was so worried about our privacy, she would have thrown me out on the spot.

Cherish's birth was a circus because of all the media. One year later, her first birthday was a circus because... well... it was a circus.

We had brought in a little circus for her party. We also had so many TV and movie stars come to the party. Dick Clark was there. Jaclyn Smith, Sally Struthers, Jane Seymour, Kenny Rogers, and my friend Herve Villechaize from Fantasy Island were all there as well! We even had the Incredible Hulk, Lou Ferrigno. All of those famous people turned out for my daughter's first birthday party. It was crazy!

In addition to the celebrities, we also had rides, clowns, jugglers, a petting zoo, dog acts, and a big cotton candy machine. And every bee in the state of California smelled that cotton candy. Thousands of them swarmed in and started stinging everyone!

I have no idea how much money I spent on that damn party, and Cherish doesn't even remember it. To make things even crazier, guess what I gave my daughter for his first birthday... I gave her a brand new corvette!

I ended up keeping that car in storage for 10 years. But then I thought, "When Cherish is old enough to drive, she will probably think, 'Why do I want this old car from 1980?'" And a corvette is not a good car to give to a teenager.

So, I sold the car, and bought savings bonds for her. Every time I made any money, I always bought a savings bond for my daughter.

That was back when savings bonds were worth something.

Charlene and I lived in Beverly Hills. Both of our careers were at their peak. Of course, Charlene continued with her acting career on 'Dallas'. She was getting $50,000 an episode! And I was traveling with Mickey Gilley at the time. We would do a concert, hop on a plane, and fly back to Hollywood. A limo would pick me up at the airport and take me home. I was truly jet-setting at the time.

I wish that everyone could experience what I was going through. Here I was, fresh out of Pasadena, Texas and the Gilley's club, and then all of a sudden I'm living in Beverly Hills, California and I'm married to a gorgeous television star!

But I quickly found out that TV stars can be a little off-the-wall. Charlene had always wanted a dog. So I got her a husky. She named it… "Goldfish"! I have no idea why.

One day, I was on the set of 'Dallas' with Charlene, and me and Patrick Duffy got in trouble. I was telling him some jokes while some of the other actors were doing a scene. Patrick started laughing so loud that the director yelled, "Cut! Knock that shit off!"

I usually played myself on most TV shows, but I was given a different part when I was on 'The A-Team'. My episode had me, Mr. T, and Boy George in it. I was cast as the leader of a group of rednecks. The script had us thinking that we were going to a George Jones concert, but it turned out to be Boy George!

Boy George was pretty different back then. He wore makeup and wore women's clothes. He is still different, but he is pretty tame compared to stuff that's going on these days. I had taken my daughter Cherish to the set with me. She was very young, and when Boy George walked in, she asked him, "Are you a boy or a girl?"

He said, "I'm a boy."

She said, "No way!"

During our two-year marriage, Charlene and I were the King and Queen of the tabloid newspapers. It seemed that they always had some kind of story about us. I'm sure that Glen Campbell and Tanya Tucker were glad that we came along, because Charlene and I helped kick Glen and Tanya off the covers of the tabloids.

The trashy stories always bothered Charlene, but they really didn't bother me that much. The paparazzi would jump out and start clicking their cameras… and she would run, but hell, I would stand and smile for them! But Charlene was starting to feel insecure, when I would have to leave to go on tour.

Charlene had some bad habits, and so did I. She decided that she wanted to get rid of some of hers, so she turned to religion. She still loves the Lord, and she is pretty religious today. She corrects my language a lot. I say stuff just to irritate the piss out of her!

One night, we were sitting on the coach watching TV, and a commercial for the National Enquirer came on. In the ad, they had an animated body with my face on it. And then, it showed me picking up a cartoon version of Charlene and throwing her in a junk pile. The ad said that I was dumping Charlene. There was no truth to the story at all. We just looked at each other. I laughed at it, but I could tell that it hurt her.

I came home from the road one day, and there were a bunch of suitcases in the living room. I asked what she was doing, and she said, "Oh, I'm getting rid of some stuff I don't need." I didn't know she was talking about me!

The next time I left the house, she moved out. She took my daughter and left.

A short time later, I was doing a show at the Palomino Club. I asked the crowd, "Does anybody have any requests?" A guy walked up with a piece of paper in his hand. I opened it, and it was my divorce papers. I was served legal papers right in the middle of my own concert!

After the show, I walked back to my dressing room. I was feeling pretty depressed, but luckily there were some girls from the 'Hee Haw' TV show there. And I ended up making a good night of it. I drowned my sorrows in some Hee Haw Honey.

I was married to Charlene for just two years. Of course, in "Hollywood years", that's a very long time.

Contrary to what the tabloids were saying, ours was not a nasty divorce.

I agreed to pay child support, Charlene didn't go after me, and I didn't go after her. It wasn't one of those bitter Hollywood divorces.

I continued living in California, even after my divorce. My daughter was there, and I couldn't imagine moving away from her. I lived on the beach at Marina del Rey. I had a bicycle, and I put a little side car on it so that I could drive Cherish up and down the beach. I found out that women would stop to talk to a guy who had a baby!

But after a couple of years, I decided that it was time for a change of scenery. I bought a place in Guntersville, Alabama, near where my road manager lived.

After I moved, and after Charlene remarried, I didn't get to see Cherish very often. And it seemed that Charlene and I were always fighting about my time with her.

Whenever Cherish would come see me, she'd always want to stay longer. And I would always say, "If you want to stay, then stay." That would make Charlene and her new husband mad. That also led to Charlene cutting back on the times that she would let Cherish come see me.

On Cherish's 14th birthday, Charlene had planned a big birthday party for her. But Cherish had been in Branson, Missouri with me, and she called her mom to tell her she wanted to stay longer.

That made Charlene so angry that she took all of Cherish's presents back to the store, and she even threw away her birthday card.

Another time, Cherish was with me when she called her mom. She said, "Daddy's cat just had kittens. Can I have one?"

Charlene said, "Absolutely not!" But when Cherish asked me if she could take one home, I said "Sure." When Cherish got off the plane, her mom yelled, "Whatever is in that crate had better be dead!"

But Cherish named the cat "Tabby", and it lived to be 18 years old. It even ended up living with Charlene after Cherish graduated high school!

I didn't talk to Charlene very much over the next decade. And when we did talk, it usually consisted of me asking her to let me spend more time with my daughter... and of her saying "No".

But over time, a little healing started to take place between us. And things got even better after she got rid of the second guy that she married. I never did like him. He was a real jerk. I always wanted to take a baseball bat to him. I'd always thought he was just after her money... and mine.

In 2009, Cherish crashed her motorcycle. It was a bad accident. She skinned her face all up. It knocked out her teeth. It took her a year to be able to walk with no pain.

When Cherish was in the hospital, Charlene called and told me that she would like me to come be with her. That was really the beginning of Charlene and I communicating again, and it was the start of us getting our friendship back.

Today, I talk to Charlene all the time. We laugh and joke a lot, and we are good friends. I had a date a few years ago, and Charlene was at my house when my date came over. It was a little awkward, but kind of fun. I asked her, "Are you sure you're not filming some hidden camera sitcom here?

CHAPTER TEN

Ricky Dies… and Sherwood Lives

When disk jockeys interview me, they almost always ask, "When you were listening to music as you growing up, who influenced you?" That's easy…

Ricky Nelson was my biggest influence.

Ricky is the one who got me interested in music.

I used to watch Ozzie and Harriet. Ricky would always screw something up each week, and then by the end of the show, he would always sing a song and get the girls. I said, "I want to do that." I was already pretty good at the screwing up part… I just had to master the music part!

I met Rick when he played at Gilleys, and I got his blessing to record 'Country Party'. It was a country version of his big hit, 'Garden Party'.

I ended up recording a couple more of Rick Nelson's songs. I did 'It's Up to You'. James Burton, who was the original guitar with Ricky, was the guitar player when I recorded Rick's songs. And James played it in the same key, with the same licks, on the same guitar.

The night Rick Nelson died… December 31, 1985. I cried that night.

Rick had a New Year's Eve show in Dallas, Texas, where he was supposed to play for the Dallas Police Association at the Park Suite Hotel. I was also booked in Dallas that night.

But Ricky never made it to Dallas. He had taken off in a small private plane from Guntersville, Alabama. Jerry Lee Lewis had owned the plane before Ricky. And it had a history of mechanical problems. Ricky's plane crashed in De Kalb, Texas.

Just before our concert started, I got word that he had been killed in the crash. I went ahead and did my show, but after our concert, I went to the hotel where he had been scheduled. I took my band with me, and we did Ricky Nelson songs. We didn't get paid anything for it, but I wanted to do it as a tribute to him. I loved the guy.

It was very surreal. Ricky was my very first hero. And here I was, standing where he was supposed to be. We sang his fans every Ricky Nelson song that we knew.

After it was over, I went and cried. Happy New Year.

With Ricky Nelson's death, 1985 went out on a tragic note.

But 1986 came in with a bang.

On January 2nd, I filed a $15 million dollar lawsuit against my old manager, Sherwood Cryer.

Since I never had a dad, I think I kind of looked at Sherwood as a father figure. And I know that he cared about me…because he had me beat up!

One night, Sherwood found out that I had some drugs on me. He had a big cop at Gilley's beat me up. Right after that, I had to go on stage and sing. I knew that Sherwood was trying to help me, in his own way. He was trying to get me to straighten up. But it didn't work. You can't straighten somebody up until they want to do it for themselves. I would finally learn that lesson many years later, with two people who I loved more than anything in the world.

But I liked to party a lot in the 80s. I was hard to keep up with. Cocaine was a recreational thing. And it helped you feel ten feet tall and bulletproof. I thought I did a lot of cocaine, until I met people who really did a lot. Number one, I couldn't afford it.

I am not proud of it. I should never have done it. But I did. And I learned my lesson from it. I outgrew it. And I wouldn't do some right now, if someone offered it to me. The same thing with pot. I wouldn't do any now.

But back in the Gilley's days, I would roll a big ol' joint. I would smoke it on my way to work and before I was to go on, so that I could get into the party mood. I would smoke it in my car. I'd keep my windows up and airtight. I would sometimes wonder if I was really high, or if I was just dizzy from holding my breath! If you would've seen me in my car in the parking lot, it would have looked like a Cheech and Chong movie. I didn't want to open the door until I had breathed in all of that shit.

Before we get to the serious stuff concerning my lawsuit against Sherwood Cryer, let me tell you a few funny stories about the man who created Gilley's...

When some of the cowboys and oil workers would come to Gilley's, some would hide their whiskey bottles outside. They'd put them on the ground next to the building. They'd bring their own so that they wouldn't have to spend money on buying it in the club, and whenever the band would take a break, those guys would go out and drink their whiskey.

Sherwood found out about it, and he'd go piss in the bottles.

Later, he made a rule that if you left the club, you had to pay another cover charge in order to get back in.

Sherwood had a bunch of illegal Mexicans working for him.

He used to put as many of them as he could in an old ice machine that was in the back of his pickup. He would drive them from job to job that he had.

One day, they were pouring concrete for his recording studio, and they were getting it leveled out when the border patrol showed up. Those illegals took off running everywhere! It looked like an ant bed! Sherwood was trying to get them out of there while he was trying to smooth the concrete before it dried out.

They used to have one night a week at Gilley's that was "$5

night". For $5.00, you got a plastic cup, and you could fill that cup with beer all night. They were pretty thin and flimsy cups. They weren't like the nice red Solo cups that we have today.

At the end of the night, when everyone left, the dance floor would be covered with those cups. Sherwood would have his Mexican crew go pick them all up, and then he would rinse out the cups and re-use them the next night. He didn't want to buy new ones.

Sherwood wanted me to learn the old song 'Pistol Packin' Mama'. but I didn't want to sing the song. Sherwood came up and stuck a pistol in my ribs. He said, "Hey asshole, get up there and do that damn song." I thought it was ironic that a guy had a pistol aimed at me as he requested 'Pistol Packin' Mama!'

I had the number one song in the country. 'Lookin' for Love' was hotter than a pancake. We flew into Houston, Texas. Sherwood picked us up at the airport. And all he had was his old pickup truck!

He put us in the truck. Mickey Gilley, Sherwood, and his son and daughter were all in the front cab. And me and the band had to sit in the back bed of that truck, all the way across Houston! I was so mad. I was embarrassed. He used to pull that shit on us all the time. He said it "kept us grounded".

To help promote the club, Sherwood bought a huge hot air balloon. Of course, it had "Gilley's" on it, in big red letters that were about 25 feet tall.

Sherwood, Mickey and I were all looking at the balloon when Sherwood said, "Johnny, let's go for a ride."

Gilley said, "You're crazy if you go with him, Johnny. He will kill you."

Sherwood had never flown a balloon by himself, but I went ahead and jumped into the basket with him.

As we lifted off, Mickey was shaking his head, saying, "Johnny, don't go!"

As soon as we had lifted off, Sherwood steered us almost right into some power lines. Next, we almost hit a hospital that was just down the street from Gilley's.

Then the wind blew us right over the Hobby International Airport. Planes were taking off and landing and here we were with this balloon that said "Gilley's"!

Of course, Sherwood had his Mexican workers all chasing us to see where we would land.

A few minutes later, I could see the Astrodome come into view.

Sherwood yelled, "We really need to put this thing down!"

I thought, "we are either going to land on the highway and get run over by a car, or we're going to slam into the Astrodome. Either way, we are probably going to end up on the TV news tonight."

Sherwood was messing with the collapse cord and the burner, as we started falling fast.

As the ground kept getting closer, I thought, "maybe I can jump up into the air as soon as we get ready to hit the ground". But it didn't work.

Luckily, we crashed in a field, and we didn't hit anything but the ground. But it is still a wonder that I am alive.

Those are some of the funny things that happened with Sherwood Cryer. But then, the laughter stopped. This is where things began to go wrong.

I had been singing at Gilley's for eight years before 'Urban Cowboy' came along. During that time, I was just a country boy with no knowledge or experience in the ways of the music business. And since I knew I didn't know much about the business, I put all of my trust in Sherwood Cryer. Sherwood was also a country boy, but I had seen how he went from being a plant shift worker to the owner of the biggest nightclub in the world. He was a sharp businessman, and to be honest, he was also like a father figure to me… a father I'd never had.

I should have stayed fatherless.

I signed a contract with Sherwood. It said that he would take care of everything for me. I never had to worry about my money. With him as my manager, all my money went directly to Sherwood. This included the money that I had made on all of my sold-out tour dates with Mickey. When I did a concert, and I was doing one every night of the week, I never saw any money from it. The check from the concert promoter went directly to Sherwood. This also included checks that came in from my gold single and album for 'Lookin' For Love'. And it included all of my songwriting royalties. All of that money was sent directly to my manager. Sherwood told me he would take care of all my money.

Even at the height of my fame, I was never a big spender. I didn't need much. So, each week, Sherwood would give me an "allowance" from my money, and he would put all of the rest "in my account".

A closer look at the contract I'd signed with Sherwood makes me cry even more. He said that he had me under a 99-year contract. That meant that I had to work for him forever. And the contract also had Sherwood getting 50% of everything I made! That was a pretty bad deal for me. But even if I had gotten just my 50%, I would be pretty well-to-do right now.

So, under our contract, Sherwood got half of the money for himself, and he was also "taking care" of my half of the money.

When I was going to marry Charlene Tilton, I wanted to buy a horse ranch in California. It was going to be the first major purchase I made after I had become "rich and famous". I had planned to buy the ranch from Snuff Garrett, who was a producer in California. But when our deal fell through, I ended up getting sued for not following through with it. I wanted to buy the ranch, but I found that I couldn't.

I went to Sherwood, and asked for some of my money so that I could buy the property.

Sherwood said, "You ain't got no fuckin' money."

He just stared at me.

I was in shock. I had dedicated my whole life to my career. I was now a big star, with hit after hit. I was gone on the road all the time. I was working my butt off, singing to huge crowds every night. But Sherwood said I hadn't made any money! I actually thought he was joking, but as he sat there glaring at me, I realized that he was serious. I couldn't believe it.

He is the only guy I have ever wanted to kill. I even dreamed about ways of doing it so I could get away with it. I thought about getting a huge icicle and stabbing him in the head. And when that icicle had melted, my fingerprints would have melted away, and there would be no evidence.

I really wanted to hurt him.

He said he had spent all the money "on my career".

It was bullshit. I had made a lot of money.

He pulled the same thing with Mickey Gilley. Gilley and I were traveling everywhere together. We used the same band, the Urban Cowboy Band, for both of our shows. We were the two hottest stars at the time, and we were using the same band so that Sherwood could save money. I even played rhythm guitar behind Mickey, when we first started.

I left Sherwood first. I told Mickey, "If you've got any sense, you will leave him." But Mickey said it was too big of a risk, and that he was going to stay with Cryer.

That's the only time Gilley and I ever got cross ways.

When I left Sherwood, I had to get an attorney; I ended up with two in California. And I paid them a butt-load of money, before I found out that they didn't have any jurisdiction in Texas. So I had to get another attorney in Texas in order to get out of my contract. Sherwood ended up taking my Mercedes, and he got all the songs that I had written. I had written some great songs, some on an album that ended up being a gold album. But Sherwood got all of the money from those songs. I never saw a dime from those.

I didn't know you could make good money writing songs. All of that money went to Points West Publishing, which Sherwood owned.

He never did pay anybody. He wanted them to be dependent on him. He didn't want you to be independent at all.

When I finally broke away from Sherwood, I thought that I could start making some money back by doing concerts. I was still selling out anyplace I went, but I quickly found out that Sherwood was still calling the shots.

When 'Urban Cowboy' hit, Mickey and I were being booked by the prestigious William Morris Agency. But good ole Sherwood broke that contract, and told us to sign with 'In Concert' booking. We did. We had no idea that Sherwood had become the new owner of 'In Concert'! My God. Now he could take his manager's fee, and then a booker's fee on top of that. He had it made.

While Mickey and I played the remaining dates that had been booked by William Morris, we never saw any of that money. Sherwood took it all. To add insult to injury, Cryer also never paid William Morris their commission… so guess who they sued for $20,000… Johnny Lee.

Of course, after I told Sherwood I was leaving him, my concert bookings through 'In Concert' quickly took a nosedive. He wouldn't book me. Cryer still had control over me. I ended up having to sell my bus, and was forced to let all my band members go.

Just after I had filed my lawsuit against Cryer, he counter-sued me. He had no legal basis to sue, but he knew that I would go broke trying to defend his suit. So we ended up settling both cases out of court. I ended up with basically nothing.

Mickey would have better luck. Shortly after I left, Mickey started noticing how rundown the club was getting. He repeatedly asked Cryer to fix it up, but Cryer responded with, "Oh yeah, now that you've been playing those big fancy places in Vegas, your own club ain't good enough for you."

Mickey finally asked him to take the name Gilley's off of the building, and Sherwood answered, "You change YOUR name."

Mickey said, "I'll see you in court." He asked me to be a character witness against Sherwood, and I said, "Absolutely."

They set the court date, and then they moved it. And they set another date, and they ended up changing that one. When they finally went to court, I had two concerts booked. And I could not get out of those.

I told Mickey I couldn't be there as a witness for him, and he took it really hard. He thought that I had abandoned him. And that was not the case at all. It broke my heart that I couldn't testify for him.

He won the lawsuit against Sherwood, however, even without my testimony.

During the court proceedings, everyone found out that Sherwood had signed Mickey to a ten-year contract. After the decade was up, Sherwood had let the contract expire, but he still wanted to keep Mickey. So he added another year to the official paper contract without telling him. Sherwood copied the contract and sent it in the mail, acting like he had picked up his option to extend Mickey's agreement, but Mickey's attorney was able to catch the change that had been made to the contract.

The judge threw the contract out, and Mickey knew he had Sherwood beat. Mickey was awarded $18 million. But hopefully he didn't go on a big shopping spree just after the verdict... because he never got the money. Mickey ended up getting less than $2 million. He got some property, the King Air plane, the buses, and an 18-wheeler, but there were so many taxes still owed on everything that it really wasn't worth that much.

Sherwood closed Gilley's in 1989, and declared bankruptcy. In March of that same year, Cryer said someone broke into the club and stole all of the equipment from the club's recording studio.

And mysteriously, right after that, Gilley's burned down. It burned right to the ground. It was all gone. It was kind of hard to comprehend. After all of the years at Gilley's, all of the music, all of the country legends, all of the fans, all of the good times, all of the tourists, all of the movie stars, all of the magic... it was all gone. Just a heap of ashes. There was nothing left.

People ask me if I think arson was the cause of the fire. My answer: Hell yes. A tin building sprayed down with foam insulation is kind of hard to catch fire by accident. Yeah, it was arson. It was never proven, but come on.

Sherwood Cryer died in 2009. He was 81 years old. At the time of his death, a reporter asked for my reaction. This is my exact quote:

"We all had our differences, but he was the one who made Gilley's operate like it did. He pulled a lot of strings for me and Mickey Gilley. He made a lot of things happen. He and I had a lot of laughs and a lot of arguments. My sympathy to his family."

Towards the end of his life, I actually went and did a show for Sherwood. I had let it all go. I couldn't live with the hatred I had for him anymore. I had to finally forgive him.

CHAPTER ELEVEN

Cherish

My marriage to Charlene only lasted for two years, but she and I did do one thing right… our daughter Cherish.

Cherish was always a Daddy's girl. We've always been close. She was a tomboy. She was a little Johnny Lee. She was stubborn. And she was always very protective of me.

Cherish is so talented. She has so many talents. She is a great artist. She likes to create things. She makes decorative things out of deer antlers. She's a great painter, she's a good writer, and she is a very good singer. But most importantly, she is a really great person.

When Cherish was four years old, I got her a little dog that looked like Toto from The Wizard of Oz. I once came back from a fishing trip and I put a big fishing cooler in the yard. The ice was melting in the cooler and turning to water. I was taking a nap, and Cherish decided to give her dog a bath… in that cooler full of freezing ice water! I woke up and said, "Why is that dog shaking?"

An hour later, I went outside to do some work, and little Cherish came up to me and said, "Daddy, I have some water for you."

She gave me the glass and I said, "That is so nice. You are such a thoughtful little girl." I drank the water, and then I started looking at it. I said, "Where did you get this?"

"Out of that red thing," she said, pointing to the cooler where she had just given the dog a bath!

When you are an entertainer, you have to miss a lot of family events. And since I was on the road all the time, I missed many of Cherish's birthdays and school plays.

One of my big regrets is that I missed her graduation. At the time, it was hard to get information from Charlene, and by the time she'd told me when the graduation was, I was already booked for shows in

Lubbock, Texas. I would have gotten sued if I'd cancelled the concerts, so I missed my daughter's graduation ceremony.

I tried my best to make up for all my absences.

On her 25th birthday, I sent her two plane tickets to El Paso. She called me and said, "Why do I need to go to El Paso, and why are they one-way tickets only?"

I said, "I want you to come see me, and you don't need a ticket back, since you will be driving your new car." I gave her a really nice car for her birthday that year.

When Cherish told me she was going to get married, she said she wanted her wedding to be at the famous Southfork Ranch. Southfork is a real ranch in Texas, but of course the ranch was made famous as the home of the Ewing family on the 'Dallas' TV show.

Since Charlene played Lucy Ewing, Southfork had always been near and dear to her. And since this would be the first time that she and I would get together again at a public event after our big divorce, the wedding promised to be quite the spectacle. And it lived up to that billing. Charlene and I both walked our daughter down the aisle together (there's a picture for you, National Enquirer!).

We called the wedding 'The Gathering'. I called it a joke. I told Cherish, "This ain't going to last. This guy is not the one for you. It ain't going to work." I went along with it and paid $5,000 to help pay for the wedding, but I was right. The marriage did not last very long. As a matter of fact, later that same year, Cherish got married to another guy! Her second wedding of 2014 was held on Christmas Eve. She wanted me to come to it, but I said, "I've already been to one of your weddings this year. I'm not driving down on Christmas Eve." But I like the husband that she has now. And I know he will be a good husband for her.

One day I was talking to Cherish on the phone, and at the end of our call, she said, "Peace to your mother."

I said back, "Well, piss on your mother!"

She yelled, "That is not what I said!" And now it has become a joke with us. When we talk on the phone, she'll say, "I love you, Papa Bear."

And I will say, "I love you, daughter. Piss on your mother." We are one unique family.

And our family is growing! In March of 2016, Cherish told me that she was pregnant. I asked her if she was sure it was hers!

A few weeks later, I was asked to play the Grand Ole Opry, and for the first time, I had my daughter sing with me on that stage. It was wonderful. She sang Lane Brody's part of 'The Yellow Rose' with me.

As we were singing, I was thinking, we have three generations up here on the Opry stage. Me, Cherish, and that little baby inside her. It was cool.

Cherish was nervous to be on the Opry, so I walked behind her and goosed her to loosen her up so that she wouldn't be so uptight. It was fun. She did a great job. It was quite an experience.

That same week, we were singing at The Nashville Palace, and again, we were singing 'The Yellow Rose'. The house band was playing for us. They were great, but they were playing the song so fast, we could barely keep up with them! And we both started laughing. We were laughing so hard, Cherish started crying and we couldn't even finish the song. The band kept going, but we were just laughing our heads off. Of course, she was pregnant, and when the song ended, she said, "I just peed a little."

I said, "We need a mop up here."

When Charlene was pregnant with Cherish, I had heard that it was good for babies to listen to music when they are in the womb, so I bought a tape of Leona Boyd, one of the world's greatest classical guitarists, for her. We put the cassette player on Charlene's stomach and played the tape over and over.

And this past year, when Cherish was carrying my grandson, I found a CD copy of that same Leona Boyd album. Cherish laid her headphones on her stomach until her belly got too big! Then she just put it into the CD player, and turned it up really loud.

My grandson's name is Wyatt Rein Christopher. That means "little warrior, guided by Christ".

When my daughter first told me the name, I said, "You should add the letter 'B' in between his first and middle name. Then I could always say, 'Why it be rainin?!'"

I could go on and on about my daughter. But when she found out I was writing this book, she said she had some things that she wanted to say. So, I will let her have the rest of this chapter.

"I call my dad 'Papa Bear'.

I was always a daddy's girl. As I was growing up, whatever mom said 'No' to, Dad would say 'Sure' to. Ear piercings, tattoos... it was all fine with him. And he taught me how to spit!

He is the one person who I can tell anything to. I can talk to him about anything. Sometimes kids have to be careful with their parents, but I can be really open with him. I can tell him things that I wouldn't even tell my mother. He stood by me when I got divorced. He has never judged me. He has always loved me.

Every child wants the approval of their parents. The fact that he asked me to sing on the Opry with him... I knew that he believed in my talent. I love going on the road with him.

There is never a dull moment with my dad. We have so much fun together, and I love him so much. Thanks to my mom and dad, I have been able to see the world.

Dad and I have a running joke about Splenda. Someone once put a box of it in the refrigerator and he got all worked up over it. He yelled, "Who puts a damn box of Splenda in the fridge?! What the hell?!"

After he left the room, I took the box and spread the packets in his bed. From that point on, I have surprised him by putting that Splenda box everywhere from inside his boots to his suitcase. He has carried that box to so many different states!

A couple of years ago when he was on the road at Christmas, I decorated his entire house and Christmas tree with individual Splenda packets!

One of my funniest memories of Papa Bear was the time he was driving and me and my brother Johnny were riding in the car. I put a song on and my brother turned it up very loud. We were both singing along, also very loud.

Dad finally yelled, "Damn it! Turn that shit down! I can't see!"

Johnny and I started laughing so hard that we were actually crying.

Even though my mom and dad divorced more than 30 years ago, I have no doubt that they still love each other. Here's a funny example…

Dad was dating a woman, and we gave her the nickname "Four Wheeler". I was dating a guy, and since he liked beer, we gave him the name "Six Pack".

Mom didn't like my boyfriend or Dad's girlfriend, so she went to her prayer group and told all the women in the group, "I just don't think this woman is right for Johnny, and I know for a fact that this guy ain't right for Cherish. So let's pray to the Lord that 'Six Pack' and 'Four Wheeler' will find each other and make the perfect couple… so they will get out of our lives!"

After their famous marriage and very public divorce, people always ask me how my parents get along today. They get along very well. Sometimes too well! One example…

Mom will come with me to stay at Dad's house in Branson. It's so funny to see them together now. The last time we were there, it was mom and dad, and me and my husband.

We were all drinking wine, and dad started playing his guitar. It was getting late, and mom kept saying, "Johnny, play another song. Play another song." When he got done, she said, "OK, let's go to bed." Dad's eyes got so big! I looked at them and said, "No more wine! Mom, you go to your room downstairs. Dad, you go to your room upstairs!" It was pretty funny, with the 30 year old daughter having to separate the parents!

When I found out I was pregnant, he was my first phone call. I called him even before I called mom.

He happened to be at a bar watching some of his buddies sing. I told him, "I just want you to know that you've got a grandbaby on the way." I told him, "This is just for family right now. So if you could just keep it quiet…" and before I could even finish that sentence, the whole bar knew I was having a baby! He was yelling, "Cherish is going to have a baby! I'm gonna be a grandpa!"

And he told most of the family before I could tell them. I did manage to tell my mom just in the nick of time, because right after that, he put it on his Facebook page! My best friend Natasha called me and said, "Hey girl! Cats out of the bag!" I said, "What cat?! What bag?!"

So I had to make a shotgun announcement to all of social media that there were some major changes that had taken place in my life. I was no longer with my ex-husband. I had married a wonderful man and we were having a baby!! All of this within year!

I know Papa Bear will spoil his grand baby. He will be a wonderful grandpa. You watch him around kids, and he is so good with them. He just melts when he is around children. But I told him, "You have to watch your mouth around that baby! I don't want my baby's first word to be a cuss word!"

Through my pregnancy, he would send my baby letters and gifts. He didn't address them to me; he always put Wyatt's name on the package.

Dad is not a typical father. He is very unique. But he is perfect for me. I love him with all my heart. Dad was really my hero when I was a little girl, and he is still my hero today. I'm so thankful for who he is in my life and now my son's life. And I'm looking forward to the next chapter of our story."

– Cherish Lee

CHAPTER TWELVE

Debbie

I met Deborah Spohr in the Dallas-Fort Worth International Airport. It was June of 1985. She was a flight attendant. I was on a payphone, as I watched her walk by. She was gorgeous. And then, a couple minutes later, she walked by again. I put down the phone and ran up to her. I said, "I need your phone number."

We stood there talking in the airport. I told her that I had a concert at Billy Bob's in Fort Worth, and I invited her to come to my show.

I was the happiest guy in the world when Debbie actually showed up!

That show was the beginning of a whirlwind romance. Debbie and I dated for a year and half, and on November 14, 1986, we were married.

I never actually asked Debbie to marry me until we were at the altar.

Even though I had not officially proposed, Debbie just kind of started planning our wedding and I went along with it. I was playing in a golf tournament in Maui, Hawaii, and she started planning for us to be married there.

When she walked down the aisle, I stopped the preacher and I whispered to Debbie, "We need to make this official. Will you marry me?"

She smiled and said, "Yes."

My friends Chris Coronado and Doc Harry served as my best men, and Debbie's matron of honor was Julie Crenshaw. She was the wife of golf great Ben Crenshaw. All the men wore white tuxedos. But just before the ceremony, Ben slipped and fell, getting huge grass stains all over his white pants.

I had a bus driver named Joe. Joe was a good ole boy from

Alabama. As he sat down for the dinner after my wedding, he said, "Boss, my food has done got cold."

I said, "That is sushi. It's supposed to be cold!"

Debbie was good for me. She was 15 years younger than me, but she acted much more mature than I did! She helped me straighten up my life a little. She helped me cut back on my drinking. We traveled the world together, and I was proud to introduce my beautiful wife to the Presidents and movie and TV stars who I was now getting to be with. We had some really great years.

But when our hard times hit, they really hit.

We were so excited when we found out that we were going to have a baby.

But Debbie was only five and a half months along when the baby came. And the tiny girl was too premature to survive. She died at birth.

I had cancelled all of my shows so that I could be with Debbie when our baby was born. I was so thankful that I was there. We were both heartbroken.

We named the little girl Heaven Lee.

We asked the people from the funeral home if they could wait to take our baby until the next morning. They agreed, and we kept our child in Debbie's room so we could all sleep together.

Early the next morning, I baptized our baby girl, and I sat and held her. A minister came in and prayed with us before they took my baby away.

Heaven was buried in Monterey, California. I helped carry the little casket with my baby at her funeral. It was the hardest thing I have ever had to do.

I had no idea that there would be more days, even harder still, to come.

Debbie brought out the best in me. She helped to bring me back from a very low point in my career and in my life. She was everything I needed. She was calm, she was very family-oriented. She really loved me, and I loved her. She helped me to start to trust people again. After I had been burned so badly by Sherwood and a few others, it took a long time for me to trust many people.

But I don't think that Debbie ever got over the death of our child. She had a real hard time as she tried to deal with the death of our baby girl. She went through a lot of bad times.

But we also had some great times. The greatest came when we found out that Debbie was pregnant with another child.

But we were very worried, when the doctors told us that the baby was going to be premature. After losing our first child during a premature birth, we knew that this could also end in heartbreak.

When Deb was seven months along, the doctors put her in the hospital. They told her she would have to stay there until the baby was born, probably a month later.

While Debbie had to stay flat on her back, I stayed in the hospital with her. I read the entire Bible during that time. That was the first time I ever read the Bible the whole way through, and I found out that the Bible was the best book ever written. It really gave me the strength that I needed at that time.

I had lost one child, and now we were fighting for another one. We would win that fight when our baby was born. A baby boy! I thought I would be original and name him "Johnny Lee II"! My son was the love of my life.

Debbie loved our new baby boy. And I loved the family we had become. Debbie's love for me helped bring me back to all of my family. She helped me to reconnect and get closer with my brothers and sisters, and she was such a beautiful person with such a beautiful spirit. That's why the next few pages are so hard to write.

Things in my marriage started to go bad when Deb stopped traveling with me. As I toured the country, she stayed at home, worrying that I was cheating on her.

She was very insecure. She thought that I screwed every girl I talked to. She didn't trust me. I might be talking to a woman, but that didn't mean that I was sleeping with them.

This was before cellphones, and my phone bill would be over $1,000 a month just from her trying to track me down. When I was on tour and she couldn't reach me, she would call the highway patrol or state police and have them try to find me. It got crazy. But I really loved Debbie.

I would go out and work my butt off. I'd try to pay the bills and make a good living. But she just did not trust me.

And then Deb started to lose her hearing. She got a disease that was a very rare, genetic thing. The doctors said that it was quite rare for a young woman like her to get that disease, but her hearing got bad, and then it got worse. And then, it just went away completely. It was gradual.

At first, we really couldn't tell what was happening. We thought, "Is she really going deaf, or is something else going on?" But then she got that lisp that deaf people have, and you could tell that her hearing was completely gone. She was totally deaf. That was one of the saddest things in the world. Here she was, married to a husband who wrote and sang songs, and she couldn't hear them.

Debbie started taking prescription pills for that problem. She was also taking pills for another condition.

When she was a flight attendant, she had been on a flight that had a lot of turbulence. It really threw her around, and she hurt her back. She was hurt so bad that it basically ended her flying career.

She started taking pain pills for it, and this was back before anyone knew that pain pills were so addictive. By the time the doctors realized that she was addicted to the pills, that addiction had just taken control of her.

A lot of our marital problems had to do with those drugs. We finally divorced, after 13 years of marriage. I got custody of Johnny, and my sister Jan moved in with me to help take care of him.

Once, Debbie came, took our son, and ran off. She ended up getting arrested in Florida.

After our divorce, I was still trying to get her back into my son's life. I wanted her to be a mom to him. But she was hooked on these damn prescription drugs. So many people are hooked on those today.

Debbie ended up stealing prescription pads, and she kept getting arrested. The last time she got put in jail, when she got out, she came to stay with us. She stayed a couple days, but then she said that she had to go. I knew what was up, and I knew that she was going to get more drugs. I told her, "Deb, the next time you get arrested, don't call me."

Sure enough, she was arrested again, and she called me. And our son said, "Dad, don't get her out. She's going to do the same thing when she gets out."

My mother came to Branson to help me raise my son. I had full custody of JL, but when I was on the road, my mother was in charge of him at home. Debbie just could not get off the drugs, and anytime she wanted to see JL, she had to ask mom, and mom also went with JL most of the time that he was with her.

On November 7, 2002, I had just taken my son to school. He was in 6th grade at the time. And when I got home, my phone rang. It was the sheriff. He told me that Deb had committed suicide. She had hanged herself in her jail cell. I hit the floor. I fell to my knees. The first thing I thought was, "how am I going to tell my son that his mother is dead?"

I called a psychiatrist, and he told me to bring Johnny in to tell him there.

I went to the school and told the principal that I needed to pick up my son. He asked me why, and I just lost it. I had to try to compose myself before Johnny got to the office.

I waited until we'd gotten to the psychiatrist's office before I told him that his mom was gone. The hardest thing that I have ever had to do was tell my son about his mother. Then, I watched as my son helped carry his mother to her grave.

I never dreamed that I would lose my wife to drugs. But I did.

Debbie was only 41 years old. She was one of the most beautiful women in the world. She was also one of the smartest and most talented women I have ever met. But drugs led to her hanging herself in a jail cell. If that could happen to her, it can happen to anyone. You need to remember that, the next time you take a pill.

Mom holding me with my Uncle Jimmy, 1946.

My stepdad Jim Linkey, Mom, Me, Claudia, Lynn, 1950.

Johnny (on left) and my brother, Lynn, 1949

Having fun at a picnic with my brother, Lynn (on left).

Lynn, Claudia, Johnny, 1951.

Lynn, Johnny, and Claudia, Galveston, Texas, 1951

Six years old in our front yard in Alta Loma, Texas

Taking a swim with brother Lynn and sisters Claudia, Janice and Janet.

First grade Alta Loma Elementary School

Dodger Days - I'm on the front row, 3rd from the left.

Nine years old after I made the
Little League All Star team.

Little League Baseball was my first love

Little League team pic. I'm on the front row, second from the left.

Fifth Grade

Sixth Grade

Four generations of my family. I'm on the floor on the left. My brother Lynn is next to me. In back Claudia, Mom, Grandpa Wilson, Great grandma and Great grandpa Wilson, Janice and Janet.

Eighth Grade

Tenth Grade

My first band - The Roadrunners

The Roadrunners (left to right) Joe Ybarra, George Buthume, Bobby Holder, Me, Claude Summeral

The Roadrunners sing at the 1962 Valentine's Dance at Santa Fe Jr. High School. Wade Hunt is on far right. Sandra Skillman is on far left.

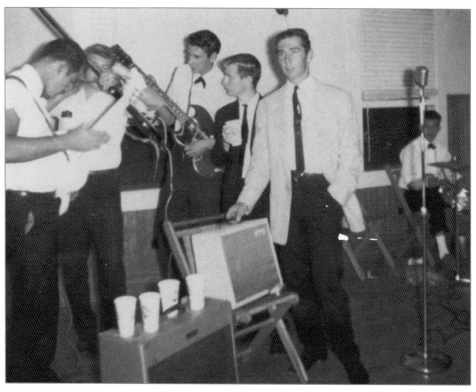

Johnny Lee and The Roadrunners - 1961

18 years old at boot camp - 1964.

A picture I sent home to my family, August 2, 1964.

Home on leave, 1965. With my little brother Jimmy and sister Janet.

20 years old - Standing in front of the missile launcher on the USS Chicago.

The Bondsman, October 22, 1965. Aboard the USS Chicago. I'm playing drums as I sit in front of a guided missile!

Navy - 1968

Vietnam - Sitting in the door of a helicopter, age 20.

The future Urban Cowboy.
More Urban than Cowboy in this one.

One of my first promotional 8x10s.
I autographed it to my mom.

Very early promo pic, before the hat and beard.

With my brothers, sisters, and mom. (Left to right) Janice, Claudia, Jimmy, Lynn, Mom, Janet, Me.

With Faron Young
January 24, 1973

With Conway Twitty
Before his perm and before my beard

The Nesadel Club, where it all started.

The Nesadel is changed to 'Johnny Lee's'

At Gilley's 1979

Clowning with Mickey Gilley. Courtesy Kirk West

Playing piano at Gilley's

With Mickey Gilley and John Travolta, 1979.

With John Travolta during the filming of Urban Cowboy.

The Gilley's hot air balloon

On stage with Mickey

Sherwood Cryer (left) keeps a close eye on my armadillos Eeny and Meeny. There ain't no Mo!

Halibut fishing in Alaska

Singing 'Dead skunk in the middle of the road' with Mickey.
Courtesy Brad Bassett

Steve Howe presenting me with my Gold Record for Lookin for Love.
Courtesy Ken Edwards

Fantasy Island TV show with Hervé Villechaize and Mickey.

With Mickey, Hervé Villechaize and Mike Schalaci

Monkeying around (Courtesy Ian Tilbury)

Performing on The Mike Douglas Show with Mickey.

With Charlene just before our wedding. February 1982.

Academy of Country Music Awards with David Frizzell and Charlene

The Star magazine got the exclusive photos of our wedding

Since the National Enquirer didn't get our wedding pictures, a few months later they said we were divorcing!

Family photo shoot for the US magazine cover, May 1983

Holding my baby daughter just after we brought Cherish home.

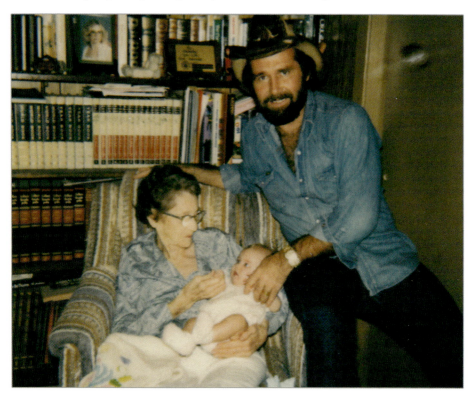
Great Grandma Wilson holds Cherish, 1983.

With Charlene at the Beverly Hilton Hotel, Nov. 17, 1983.
Photo courtest Scott Downie

Celebrating my ACM Most Promising Male Artist Award with Bill Boyd

John Boyland, the man who produced *Lookn' for Love* and *Cherokee FIddle*

In London 1983 making sure that
Big Ben had the correct time.

A wild night on stage at Gilley's with Johnny Paycheck

Dodger Days again. Rick Sutcliffe and Steve Howe, 1982.

With baseball legend Billy Martin. He let me wear his World Series ring for the night.

Visiting with TV's Kojak Telly Savalas

With Grandmother Wilson on her 80th birthday.

Playing at the Houston Astrodome.

With Mom

With Tony Orlando and my mom in Lake Tahoe

Mom, me, Aunt Mary, Uncle Charles

Proud Papa with Cherish

My daughter Cherish joins me on stage

With Roger Miller

With Sylvia and Roger Miller

With Comedy Legend Red Skelton

With Sammy Davis Jr. and Mickey

One of my best friends, Bubba Rigby

With my pals TG Sheppard and Moe Bandy

My little buddy
Danny Cooksey

With Glen Campbell and Charley Pride

CHAPTER THIRTEEN

Colon Cancer - A Real Pain in the Ass

Have you ever had God talk to you? I have. He told me, "You need to go to the doctor."

In 2002, I was feeling good. I felt totally healthy. It had been a long time since I had gotten a physical, and I really had no reason to go to the doctor. But I know that it was God talking to me, telling me to go to the doctor.

So, just out of the blue, I called them and set up an appointment. I asked for a complete physical, and they said it would include the standard test for colon cancer. That's the test that most of us men dread more than anything.

As I leaned over the table, the doctor ran his finger up my ass. I told him, "Gee Doc, I didn't bring you flowers or even buy you dinner yet."

A short time later, my doctor called and told me that I should come back in to talk to him. That's usually not a good sign.

I was on my way to go fishing. I had my son and his two buddies with me. I was driving us all in my truck. I told them to wait in the truck, and that I'd be right back after I talked to my doctor.

As soon as I walked in, my doctor told me, "You are in the beginning stages of colon cancer." It freaked me out. I immediately thought… Death.

Cancer is a bitch. I have seen so many of my friends get cancer. They said they were going to fight it, and they did everything they could. But sometimes, once cancer gets ahold of you, it can kick your ass.

My first question was "Am I going to die?"

My doctor told me I should have surgery as soon as possible. I told him I had some big-paying shows coming up, and I asked if I was going to die before those. He said, "No. You will be fine. But you need to have surgery in the next couple of months."

I walked back to my truck and tried to act like everything was alright. I just couldn't tell my son and his friends. But as we drove along, I kept thinking, "This is it. I am going to die."

My mother was staying with me in Branson, helping me take care of my son. When I went home, I tried to tell my mom, but I just couldn't. Finally, I said, "Mom, I have something to tell you. I have colon cancer." She cried. And I cried.

The next day, I went to the Point Royale golf course in Branson, where I had a game scheduled with my buddy Moe Bandy. Before we started, I broke the news to Moe. He told me how sorry he was, then we went on with our golf game.

We were on the Par 4 third hole. Moe thought he would hit a career 3-wood all the way to the green. It was probably the hardest drive he has ever hit. I was ahead of him on a golf cart. The guy I was with had hit his ball in the bushes. I was sitting in the cart when I heard "Whap!" And I felt a sharp pain right in between my shoulder blades. I thought I had been shot. Moe's ball had hit me right in the back. It knocked me down. I had dimples in between my shoulders that said "Titleist 4" for about eight months.

Moe came running up to me and yelled, "Johnny, Johnny, are you alright?!"

I looked up at him and whispered, "Is that all you got?"

When I had my cancer surgery, Moe was there when I came out of the operating room. When my anesthesia was wearing off, I opened my eyes and saw Moe standing over me. He said, "Johnny, this is what they took out of you during the surgery." And he gave me a little Tupperware container. I opened it, and inside was a golf ball that he had covered in ketchup!

While they didn't really take a golf ball out of me, I did have a foot and a half of my colon removed. I lost a lot of weight. But it saved my life.

After my surgery, I had a little recovery time, but it really didn't slow me down at all. I didn't cut back on my schedule, and I stayed busy out on the road. During my concerts, I would tell all the men in the audience, "Don't be macho. Go get checked out."

I think that with all the growth hormones that are used in food and animals, and all the antibiotics they put in our food, it is more important than ever before to get checked, early and often.

In 2004, I was told that I was totally cancer-free.

Now, more than a decade later, the only lingering effect that I have is I have to be careful about what I eat. I have found out that what goes in has to come out. And when I feel the need to go to the bathroom, I know I need to get there right now.

Looking back, I know that it must have been God talking to me. If I hadn't gone to the doctor when I did, I would be dead now. It saved my life. It had to have been a message from God.

And I had even more to be thankful for in the summer of 2004.

I was honored and humbled when it was announced that I would be inducted into the Texas Country Music Hall of Fame!

I became a member of the Hall of Fame alongside Mac Davis and the late JP Richardson, The Big Bopper.

I was so grateful that they did it while I was still alive, especially after my cancer battle over the last two years.

My friend John Daly flew down to the ceremony, and he was the one who gave me my Hall of Fame plaque. I passed it on to my mother, who was sitting in the crowd.

They also called President Bush on the phone, and he talked about me.

A short time later, I was visiting the Hall of Fame. A woman was standing in front of my exhibit with her little girl. The mom told her, "These are all country music stars. Most of them are dead now."

I stepped up and said, "I'm not!"

The little girl looked at my exhibit, and then looked back at me, and totally freaked out. She ran down the hall! I found her later in the gift shop, and autographed a picture for her.

It is really something, to think that my exhibit will be there from now on. They have my boots, my Texas jacket, and a cowboy hat. I had a hat with a lizard hat band. It had raccoon fur and pheasant feathers on it. Someone once asked me if a chicken had exploded on my hat!

And here's another cowboy hat story for you…

I always wore my favorite cowboy hat on all of my album covers and when I did my most important shows. My Charlie 1 Horse hat became kind of my trademark.

My hat had javelin tusks and agate stone. It also had very expensive feathers. I never let that hat out of my sight. It was worth a lot of money, and it was very special to me.

One night, I did a show in Detroit. I was riding in the back of huge limousine with some radio disc jockeys, and of course, there were a few girls in the car too.

We had been dancing and drinking, having a big time.

One of the girls asked if she could see my hat. Without thinking, I said, "Sure you can." I handed it to her, then I looked away when one of the DJs asked me a question. Right then, I heard this woman coughing and gagging. I turned back around, and she was throwing up right into my hat!

I yelled for them to stop the car, grabbed my hat and opened the door. It was raining like a son of a bitch, as I was pouring puke out of my hat. I was slinging it against the limo. I had a show the next day, I would need my hat, and it was ruined!

I knew that there weren't any cowboy hat shops in Detroit, so when I got back to the hotel, I washed it out in the bathtub. I tried to reshape it, and then I put it on the air conditioner vent to dry out. It ended up shrinking.

When I got back to Texas, I took it to be professionally reshaped, but it really never was the same. Once a hat has been soaked… and puked in… it is never the same.

CHAPTER FOURTEEN

My Country Music Friends

I have lots of friends in the country music business.

Of course, Mickey Gilley is the one who has been there from the beginning, and I am proud to say that after all these years and everything we have been through, Mickey and I are closer than friends. We are more like brothers. I love him to death.

In 2009, Mickey suffered a horrible neck and spinal cord injury. He was helping a friend move a loveseat, when he fell backwards and the coach fell on him. Mickey ended up paralyzed from the neck down. His doctors told him that he would never walk again. But he said, "No way! I am going to walk again!" And sure enough, after months of hard work, he did walk again. And not only is Mickey walking, he is performing again.

We started doing shows together again a couple of years ago, and we sold out every place we worked. Gilley is really amazing.

What kind of guy is Mickey Gilley? In the late 60s, he was paying me $90 a week. In 1980, when I got a triple platinum album, Mickey raised my pay to $100 a week! I love you, MG.

"When I see Johnny, I sometimes ask him, 'Do you want to take my picture?' That's an inside joke between the two of us. Here's what it means… Back in the 80s, we were in my King Air plane, and we were flying all over the country.

Johnny had bought a new camera, and he said, "I am going to document all of this! I'm getting it all on film. I might even turn it into a book someday!" He was taking photos, one after another, everywhere we went. He made us smile and pose, as he took his time to get just the perfect picture. He did that for a week, and then he found out that he'd never had any film in the camera!

One time, we were at a show and the girls were going crazy. As we were singing, a few of them came up to the stage and put pieces of paper with their phone numbers into our hands. I just sat the ones that I got down by the drums, but Johnny put all of his into his pocket.

After the show, Johnny met this gorgeous woman. She was unbelievable. Of course, he asked for her phone number. She gave it to him, and I watched him put it in his pocket. I knew right at that moment that he had forgotten about all the others he had already put in there!

The next day, he pulled out the number to call this beautiful woman, and when she answered, he said, 'I miss you. Would you come see me?'

She said, 'I would love to,' and he sent her a first class airline ticket.

He asked me to go with him to pick her up at the airport. We waited by the ramp, and here came this woman. She threw her arms around him as she yelled, "Johnny!" and started hugging him.

He looked at me and mouthed, "Who is this?" He had gotten the wrong phone number and invited the wrong girl to town! Only Johnny."

– Mickey Gilley

Mickey Gilley is a true gentleman, and he is my best friend. Here's a Mickey Gilley joke for you...

I was walking on the beach, when I stumbled on an old bottle. I picked it up, and a genie came flying out. The genie said, "I will give you two wishes."

I happened to have a world map that I always kept folded up in my speedos. I pulled out the map, and told the Genie, "Do you see these two countries? Iraq and Iran. I wish they would quit fighting and stop killing each other."

The genie said, "Wow. That is a pretty tall order. They have been fighting for hundreds of years. I don't know if I can handle something that tough. Do you have a second wish?"

I said, "I wish Mickey Gilley could have another number one record."

The genie stood there and said, "Let me see that map again."

Of course that's just a joke, but there really is a lot of truth to that story. The truth is... no matter how hot a country star has been... no matter how many hits they have had, or how many records they have sold... once they fall off the charts and radio stops playing them... not even a magic genie can get them another hit.

But our fans still show up to see our shows. And I am thankful for that!

Here are a few memories of some of my favorite friends in country music:

I love Crystal Gayle. One morning, on my birthday, my phone rang. I was half asleep when I answered it, and on the other end of the phone I heard the voice of an angel. Crystal Gayle was singing 'Happy Birthday' to me!

I said, "I don't need anything else for my birthday." How many people can say that Crystal Gayle woke them up as she sang to them? I hadn't even gotten out of bed yet and my birthday was already perfect.

I love T. Graham Brown. T. Graham prays for me every day. I pray for him, too. He is a sweetheart. He sings his ass off. I love his mannerisms on stage. He is like an updated Joe Cocker. His wife Sheila is also a sweetheart.

We were going on the Country Music Cruise once, and on the cruise, me and T. Graham did a live version of Family Feud. They came to one question, and before I had even gotten to see it, they took away my buzzer and microphone. They said, "We are not letting you answer this."

The question was: "Name an electrical appliance that a woman can plug into the bathroom and use."

Lane Brody is a doll. Of course, I had a number one duet with Lane on 'The Yellow Rose'.

I met Lane for the first time when we went in the studio to record that song. I liked her, and we clicked right off the bat. She was just coming off of a big hit called 'Over You', which was in the movie 'Tender Mercies'.

Lane had the 'Yellow Rose' song, and she thought that my low voice would blend in well with hers if we did it as a duet. 'The Yellow Rose' was the theme song of the TV show that starred Cybil Shepherd and Sam Elliott.

Lane was just a jewel to work with, and we did some shows together, but I wish we could have toured together more. We did another duet after that, called 'I Could Get Used To This'. It was a great song, but for some reason the promotion for the song got pulled, and we weren't able to follow up on our number one.

Lane is a great gal. A great person.

"Let me tell you about 'My Johnny'.

Johnny is one of the five men in the music business who has integrity. He never made a move on me. He was always a gentleman. He has always respected me as an artist. When we traveled together, he was always like a big brother.

I had never met Johnny until we went into the studio to record the song 'The Yellow Rose'. Of course I knew the song 'Lookin' for Love', but I didn't know Johnny at all.

Michael Zinberg was the executive producer of 'The Yellow Rose' TV series, and he wanted me to play Cybil Shepard's younger sister. He also wanted me to sing the series theme song, but he wanted me to do it as a duet. I remember that Johnny was not real enthusiastic about recording the song, but he went along with it.

Our producer in Nashville, Jimmy Bowen, was also less than thrilled about the song lyrics. He looked at them and said, "These are corny. We aren't doing it."

I asked, "If I fix the lyrics, can we do it?"

He said, "You can try to work on it, but we are going to lunch."

So I sat on Reggie Young's guitar case and I re-wrote 'The Yellow Rose'. I told Johnny, "WE wrote The Yellow Rose."

In good faith, I did that. When you see who wrote the song, it says "John Wilder, Johnny Lee and Lane Brody".

Bowen listened to my lyrics, and he loved them. We recorded the song, and everyone loved it. But the record company chose to put the song out on the 'B-side' of another Johnny song called 'Say When'. I was so disappointed!

But for some reason, the radio DJs started turning the record over and playing 'Yellow Rose'. It shocked everyone... everyone but me.

Everyone remembers the number one duet that Johnny and I had with 'The Yellow Rose', but not many people remember that Johnny and I also did a second duet. It was called 'I Could Get Used To This'.

It was a beautiful ballad, and that is my forte. I'm a ballad singer, and I love to sing those big, strong, high power ballads. I wasn't sure how Johnny would do on it, but he really rose to the occasion. His soul came out on that record like no other record that I had ever heard him do before.

I'm grateful that I know Johnny. He is like my brother."

– Lane Brody

Chris Young is one of today's big hitmakers. Chris recorded a song called 'Neon'. It has the line in it, "With a little Johnny Lee on". I thought it was so cool that they would put my name in a song.

We did the Austin County Fair in Texas together. I opened for him, and he told everyone that he didn't want to follow me. And me and my band were hot that night. We tore the crowd up. They didn't want me to leave the stage!

In between shows, Chris sent word that he would like me to come and see him on his bus. When I got there, he asked me to do a shot of Jack Daniels with him. He opened the bottle and got two shot glasses. I took both glasses in my hands and said, "We don't need these." I turned that bottle up and chugged it. I gave it to Chris and said, "It's your turn."

During his show, when he sang 'Neon', when it came to the Johnny Lee line, I walked out on stage. By that time, I was drunker than a piss ant. I held my arms open, and he thought I was going to hug him. But I walked up and kissed him right on the mouth!

Everyone in the crowd went crazy. You can find the video all over YouTube. Just search for 'Johnny Lee kisses Chris Young'. It was a good kiss too. But there was no tongue exchanged!

Rhonda Vincent is such a sweetheart. I love to watch her sing. She's got her own unique style. We were doing the 'Country's Family Reunion' TV show together, and she said, "My daddy told me if my voice ever broke into vibrato that I would go straight to hell." She is straight bluegrass.

We have become such great friends. I can't believe she gave me her phone number. I call and text her, and I have prayed for her when she was sick. She also has a great husband. Rhonda makes me laugh. I love Rhonda Vincent.

Johnny Paycheck played at Gilley's one night, and I became fast friends with him. After the show, we all drank a bunch of beer and whiskey. I went up to his hotel room, and we snorted some stuff. It was a crazy time to be a country star.

Johnny and I also wrote a great song. It was "What Started Out as Heaven for Us, Ain't Nothin' but a Living Hell". I was thrilled to write a song with him

When I met Loretta Lynn for the first time, I was actually shaking. I was so nervous. I ended up doing a bunch of shows with her. She told me, "Let me give you some advice. Write, write, write. Be writing a song all the time." She was always so sweet. I love Loretta Lynn.

Charley Pride was really into baseball. He came close to being a professional baseball player instead of a country star.

Charley was on tour with Roger Miller, and at the time, everyone was amazed that a black man could make it big in country music. One day, Charley was lying in his hotel room bed, watching a ball game. Roger Miller ran in and grabbed Charley's toes and said, "Eeny, Meeny, Miny, Moe…You take it from there Charley!" And Roger ran out of the room.

I love Charley. And I love his beautiful wife, Rozene. They both love coconut pie, and so do I. We have had so much fun together. He has always been such a great gentleman.

I was on a plane with Roger Miller, we were in first class on American Airlines, and we were flying into Albuquerque, New Mexico.

Roger was complaining about all of the hours that we had to spend on our bus. He said, "That bus is for the lower class. This is the way to go."

Right at that moment, the pilot came on the speaker, saying, "We are having a problem with our landing gear. We need to prepare for a hard landing."

When we looked out the window, we could see them spraying white foam on the runway. As Roger put his head down, he said, "Ya know, that old bus doesn't sound too bad right now."

I once did a show at the Houston Astrodome with Johnny Cash. When I met him, I felt like I was meeting true music royalty. It was almost like talking to Jesus. It totally blew me away. And Johnny was such a gentleman to me.

Mickey Gilley and I were playing at a casino in Reno. BB King was also playing there. BB was playing in a much smaller room than we were, and I thought that was odd, but that shows you how hot we were at the time.

I met BB and he said, "Come party with me after the show." I went out with him and two of his bodyguards, and we met up with Redd Foxx. Redd played Sanford on the hit TV show 'Sanford and Son', and Redd could party.

He was wearing a black fur coat, and the pockets were full of cocaine.

We stayed up all night partying. I was the only white guy there. I was thrilled just to be in BB's presence.

At daylight, me and BB walked into the Harrah's Hotel.

Quite a few years later, I took my son to Argentina. We were going hunting there; and on the flight back, BB King was also on the plane with us.

I went up to him and said, "BB, do you remember me?" He started laughing and hugged my neck. He said, "I have tried to forget about that night with Redd Foxx!"

Luke Bryan is one of the most popular guys in country music right now, but to be honest, I couldn't name you one song he does. But I know who Luke Bryan is. We did a show together. He came to meet me on my bus, and he was really a cool guy. I called him later and said, "Thank you for not being stuck-up."

Wade Hayes was my lead guitar player. In the summer of 1993, Mickey opened a Gilley's club on Music Row in Nashville. It was near the Country Music Hall of Fame, and he asked me to be the regular headliner there. They had a house band, and Wade Hayes was my guitar player.

On Wade's birthday, I took him to his first titty joint. It billed itself as having 100 beautiful women, and 3 ugly ones.

I also had Wade on the Grand Ole Opry with me. And I told the audience, "This is my guitar player Wade Hayes. Look out for him. He's going to be a big star someday."

I told him, "Brother, when you sign with a record company, don't let them change who you are." And as soon as they'd signed him, they started trying to mold him into something he wasn't. Wade is one of the most talented guys in the world. I admire him so much.

Wade ended up getting colon cancer, just like me. But he was younger than me when he got it. We never really talked about it, but when I found out that he had cancer, I prayed for him. I prayed for him a lot. And he was able to beat it, just like I did. He is a great human being.

"Yes, Johnny took me to the Deja Vue Strip Club! That was an eye-opening experience for a hayseed from Oklahoma!

I originally moved to Nashville to be a lead guitarist and a songwriter. I didn't know that I was going to be an artist. I just wanted to play guitar for somebody. That was my dream.

That dream came true when I got a job playing in the house band at the Gilley's club in Nashville. I played lead guitar for Johnny every night for more than a year, and we played five to seven nights a week.

For some reason, Johnny took a liking to me. He was very good to me. I was just a kid. I didn't know anything about anything. But he did some very nice things for me.

The first time I played the Grand Ole Opry was because of Johnny. He called and asked me to play guitar for him when he was on the Opry. It was a highlight of my life, to play on the Opry for the very first time.

This is my favorite story about Johnny: I had gotten fired from the Gilley's club. There were some record label people coming to watch me play. They got very interested in me, and they came to see me a few times. It started looking like I might get a record deal.

The management at Gilley's saw that, and they tried to get me to sign a management deal with them. I knew that if I signed it, it would mess up my possible record deal, so I refused to sign with them. So, they got mad and fired me.   It really hurt my feelings. I packed all my stuff up and I was about to leave in my truck, when Johnny ran over and stopped me.

He yelled, "What are you doing?"

I said, "They just fired me."

He said, "Go put your stuff back in the club. I will take care of this!" He came back a few minutes later, and said, "Get your ass back in there! You ain't fired."

He really stood up for me. That meant a lot to me, and I will never forget that. And I would have loved to have heard exactly what he said to that club manager!

I was thrilled to still have my job at Gilley's, but I was still swinging a hammer during the daytime as I built houses. That was my day job. But I'd play music at the club with Johnny until 2:00 in the morning. And then I had to be back building houses at 7:00 AM. That didn't leave me with much time to sleep.

But that was one of the best times of my life. And I wrote the song, 'Old Enough To Know Better' during that time, which was loosely based on that situation of playing all night with Johnny and being half awake on the job early in the morning! So in a roundabout way, he was responsible for helping me write a number one song. Chick Rains, who I wrote my first hits with, also wrote Johnny's number one song 'One in a Million' And that is still my very favorite Johnny Lee song. I never knew why Johnny liked me so much. He took me to Texas to play shows with him, and he has taken me on some country music cruises just so that I could play guitar for him.

I learned a lot just by watching Johnny's interaction with his fans. I've had the pleasure of playing with him and doing shows with him over many years now. People love him. He is great on stage, he is very charismatic, and I think the world of him."

– Wade Hayes

I was always a big Waylon Jennings fan. I met Waylon's wife Jessie Colter when we were taping Larry Black's 'Country's Family Reunion', and she and I became friends. She is so beautiful and so talented.

I played a show in Arizona once, and Jessie came out to see me. Before the show, she came onto the bus, and I asked her if she would sing a couple songs. She sang 'Storms Never Last' and 'I'm Not Lisa'. After I'd introduced her, I walked her out on stage and then I walked her off. It was one of the highlights of my life.

Seeing Jessie again reminded me of my party days. I did a big concert with Waylon in Los Angeles, and at the time, Waylon (and just about everyone else) was into cocaine. We were in a limo, and he was hiding in the floor because he thought people were trying to spy on him from up above. It was a very strange night.

Mel Tillis' drummer got drunk one night. As he was stepping off the bus, he fell and broke his nose. He went to the doctor, and asked what he should do. The doc said, "Stay off of it for a few days."

In the late 80s, I signed on to do a show with Barbara Fairchild. The show was on for four or five days a week, at a theater in Branson. Barbara is a great person, but it just did not work out.

If we didn't draw a big crowd, I would go nuts. I really took it personally. And I started to go have a few beers before I'd go out to a half empty theater. The alcohol didn't affect my entertaining a bit. I am a professional.

But Barbara and her husband pulled me aside and said, "You are forbidden to do that."

I said, "Forbidden? You don't forbid me to do something, unless you want me to go right out and do it."

I did keep my word to them, and I didn't drink anything before I went on. But just as soon as the show was over, I'd go get my beer. And I guess I got a reputation as a beer-drinker. And my show with Barbara didn't work out.

But after my son died in Branson, Barbara was very supportive. She prayed for me, and she did everything she could to help me get through it. I love Barbara.

Larry the Cable Guy came to Branson. Larry is a big fan of mine. He called me, and he was trying to sound like Barry Manilow. He said, "Hey Johnny, this is Barley Marilow. I'm a Barry Manilow impersonator," and he invited me to his show.

I ended up going with Moe Bandy and Mickey Gilley, and we all visited Larry backstage.

I noticed that when people are around comedians, the people are always trying to be funny. They will tell jokes to the comedians. I thought, "How stupid is that?" It's like going to see a great singer, and you walk up to the stage and ask them to let you sing a song.

But here I was with Larry the Cable Guy, and of course I am telling him my best jokes!

Then Larry asked Moe, "What is the strangest thing that's ever happened to you on stage?"
Moe said, "I was in Branson, and an old man and his family came backstage to meet me. And just as they were leaving, the man died. He died right there." He continued, "But that's not the strangest thing. Another time, I was in the middle of my show, and a guy in the audience died during my concert!"

Larry the Cable Guy and Mickey Gilley both sadly shook their heads. I looked at Moe and said, "Moe, it sounds to me like you need to change your set list!"

In the 80s, I became friends with a little five year old boy. I met him at Fan Fair in Nashville. I was there signing autographs, and this little red-haired kid jumped up on my table and said, "Johnny Lee, my name is Danny Cooksey, and I want to sing a song for you!"

His mom sat him up on the counter, and Danny belted out the greatest version of 'Lookin' for Love' that you have ever heard! Everyone in the place just stopped as he sang. We became buddies, and I started putting Danny on my shows.

I got him a Charlie 1 Horse hat just like I wore. He was cute as a button. All the women wanted to kiss him. He had it made!

And from all the appearances he did with me, he was seen by some people in Hollywood. Three years later, when he was eight, he became a regular on the TV show 'Different Strokes' with Gary Coleman. Danny and I are still friends today. It's hard to believe that the little guy is now 41 years old!

I played a concert with Larry Gatlin at an event called FuddFest in Gleason, Wisconsin. There were thousands of people there. I opened for the Gatlins.

As I was singing, I looked down from the stage and there were about 10 guys wearing Scottish kilts. They all lined up, right in front of the stage, with their backs to the crowd, and they were facing us. They all lifted their kilts up at the same time, and they had fake dongs that were sticking straight up! I cracked up!

After I got through singing, I went out and started visiting with everyone. A bunch of rednecks got me totally hammered on moonshine. They made me try all kinds of different moonshine and I got smashed.

By that time, the Gatlins were singing, and I walked out and gave Larry a big hug. I said, "I love you so much. I'd like to sing a song with you. I'd like to sing 'The Bitter they are the harder they fall'." Even as drunk as I was, I nailed that song! Everyone went crazy.

But since I was drunk on that moonshine, I decided to stay on stage and 'help Larry with his show'. Larry saw a bar stool on the side of the stage, and he asked if anyone had some rope. He had me sit on that stool, and then he tied me up with a bungee cord! After a couple of songs, he let me go. Only at FuddFest can you see a country star strapped down to a bar stool with a bungee cord!

I was celebrating my birthday with a special party and concert. We were also celebrating my friend John Daly's birthday. John sang with me on stage, and Doug Stone was going to come on after we were through.

But the entire time John and I were up during our show, Doug was sitting backstage, drinking Crown Royal. By the time he got on stage, there was no way that Doug could play with the backup band that we had. He tried, but finally Doug said, "Why don't you guys take a break?"

As the band was leaving the stage, the drummer picked up an urn that was near his drums. Doug asked, "What is that?"

The drummer said, "That is our former drummer, 'Shorty'. When he died, we promised we would take him to all of our shows."

Doug was almost falling off his stool, he was so drunk. He lifted up the lid of the urn, looked down, and said, "That's Shorty down there? Well it looks like he could use a drink." And he took his Crown Royal bottle and poured it in the urn!

Ronnie McDowell is a great guy. He had most of his big hits at about the same time that I had mine. He also played Gilley's quite a few times, and the girls always went crazy when he sang in his Elvis voice.

Last year, I read Ronnie's autobiography "Bringing It To You Personally". I was in an airport when I finished his book, and when I got onto the plane, I purposely left the book behind in a seat. I hoped that whoever found it would read it and get to know Ronnie and his music.

I loved his book. And it really helped motivate me to write my own book. And I ended up using the same co-author that Ronnie did.

I was golfing with Neal McCoy in Moe Bandy's tournament. Neal told me a joke.

Little Red Riding Hood was walking in the woods and she came up on the Big Bad Wolf. She looked at him and said, "My, what big eyes you have." And the Big Bad Wolf said, "Screw you bitch. I'm trying to take a dump."

So everytime I see Neal McCoy, I always tell him, "My, what big eyes you have!"

A friend asked if I knew Alan Jackson, and I told them that I really didn't. My friend told me that a little boy was dying of cancer, that he loved Alan Jackson and dreamed of meeting him.

I made a few calls, and got in touch with Alan's office, where I explained everything to them and gave them the boy's contact info.

When Alan got my message, not only did he go to the hospital, but his wife also went with him. And they held hands and prayed for that little boy.

The fact that he took the time to do that… my hat is off to Alan Jackson for making that little boy's dream come true.

Ed Bruce is one of my best friends. He took me to church. A few years ago, we were both together in Branson, and Norma Jean, who used to be with Porter Wagner, had a Sunday morning service. Cal Smith came to the service that same day.

We are playing shows on most Saturday nights, so we are traveling on most Sunday mornings, so that makes it hard to go to church. But even as crazy as I act, the Lord is still near and dear to my heart.

CHAPTER FIFTEEN

Johnny Lee the Second

When my wife Debbie and I found out that she was pregnant again, we were both so excited! I got the news when I was on the road, and we made plans for me to pick Debbie up at the Tucson Arizona airport.

When she stepped off the plane, she was met by a 250 pound baby (And one very hairy baby!)! I was wearing a baby's bib, I didn't have a shirt on, and I was holding a pacifier. I had a bed sheet that we had turned into a huge diaper! When I walked through the metal detector, the big safety pins on my 'diaper' set the machine off. I told the security agents, "If I take off these pins, we will really cause a scene."

With today's airport security, there is no way they would let a big man wearing only a diaper get through!

Johnny Lee II was born on June 4, 1990, in Monterey, California.

When he was born, I had a jeweler come in and put Johnny's tiny thumb in a warm ball of wax. And I had his thumbprint put into a heart locket. I had his birthstone put on it. I made it for his mother. After Debbie died, I took the locket and started wearing it. It might look a little feminine, but just try to take it off me. It never leaves my neck.

When he was a baby, up until he was about ten, we called him 'Little Johnny'. But as he grew up, we started calling him 'JL'.

When Little Johnny was born, I knew that I had never loved like that before. He was my whole existence. I started keeping a diary scrapbook for him before he was born, where I wrote down the details of each day up until he graduated high school. It turned into a number of scrapbooks. I've got his first movie ticket, his first airplane ticket... I wrote down his whole life story. I logged everything, the first time he took a step, things that he would say... I saved every letter he wrote. I still have it all.

When Johnny came along, my daughter Cherish kind of thought

that he was stealing her thunder. She had been the center of attention, and now here's this new kid.

She says that she thought about pushing him down the stairs, but she never followed through. As he grew up, however, they became really tight. They were close. He was her half-brother, but Cherish says that he was her other half. She really loved him.

I used to dedicate the song 'My Special Angel' to my son.

When he was a little guy, before he would go to sleep, I'd walk him around and sing 'My Special Angel'. After he got bigger, he said, "Dad, that is kind of gay. Would you stop?" I wouldn't stop.

Johnny was about ten years old when Deb and I divorced. In 2003, my sister Jan moved up to Branson to stay with us. She took care of Johnny when I was on the road, and when I was recovering from my cancer surgery.

Johnny was like me; he was kind of mischievous as a kid. He loved to laugh. He once brought a big turtle into the house, and asked me, "Do you think he bites?"

I said, "Stick your finger in his mouth and see."

"No way!" he said. He left out the door and took the turtle over to the neighbor's house. A few minutes later, the neighbor kid came running in screaming, and that turtle was still hanging on to his finger. Johnny looked at me and said, "Yeah Dad, the turtle bites!"

Johnny and his friend Danny Martinez were inseparable when they were growing up. Danny went everywhere with us. I took him to Florida with us. They both performed together in a talent show at school. They played the song 'Tequila' and they were horrible! But it was so funny.

I once played a joke on Danny. I talked him into mooning a van full of people. As soon as he pulled his pants down and put his butt to the window, I yelled, "Oh no! Here comes the state police!" He sat down as fast as he could and started looking all around for the cops. He never mooned anyone again after that!

I would buy Johnny a hundred dollars' worth of socks, but he would always take my mine. He would wear my socks all the time. I like unique socks. I have socks with penguins, and ones with eyeballs on them. My daughter Cherish also likes to wear my socks.

Johnny had such an outgoing personality. He was loved by all of his friends.

He had lots of friends. I knew those kids from the time they were in elementary school. They used to come over to my house; they would all come over and hang out, and I would cook for them. I'd always have cookies, pies or brownies, and I would always cook breakfast or dinner for them.

I would make fancy meals for his friends. I would cook some Porterhouses, or prime rib and chicken cacciatore. His buddies would love it, but Johnny always told me, "Stop being such a gourmet. Just cook regular stuff. Stop gourmet-ing all that fancy stuff."

The next time he brought four buddies over, I met them wearing a tall, white chef's hat and a chef's coat! I knew it would make him laugh.

We always called him Little Johnny, but one summer, when he was in the 10th grade, he started growing and growing, and he ended up being taller than me. And it was silly for us to call him Little Johnny after that. So, most of us started calling him JL.

JL was a great kid, but I had to go to the office at his school more than once. It was never anything serious, he never got into fights or anything. He was well-known and well-liked by all of his friends and teachers, and every girlfriend he ever had loved him so much. JL always treated his girlfriends like queens.

JL liked to play pranks. I brought a date home one night, and she was all dressed up. She went to the sink and turned on the water. You know the water squirter that is attached to your sink… JL had taped the squirter to where it was wide open, and it shot water all over my date.

One day, he walked around our neighborhood dressed in a bright yellow chicken outfit. It wasn't even Halloween! But he just liked to make people laugh.

We were driving one hot summer day, and he turned my heated car seats on when I wasn't looking. I started sweating and turned the air conditioning up. I said, "Man, it is hot today!"

He said, "It sure is!" He watched my face get redder and redder, and just as I started cussing my air conditioner, he finally burst out laughing.

Johnny was so funny. He was much funnier than I ever was. One of the funniest stories about Johnny is about the time he lost his virginity.

He and his girlfriend had both decided they would lose their virginity to one another. A few days before the big event, Johnny went to the store and bought some condoms. Then, later in the week, he went to his girlfriend's house and he quickly found out that his girlfriend's mom was the woman who had checked him out at the store when he was buying the condoms!

Johnny wanted to do music. He was a great talent, and I got him a set of drums when he was a little boy. He was a great drummer. I took him out on the road with me. He was next in line to be my drummer. He played drums on my 'Live at Billy Bob's' album. My regular drummer let him play on 'Pickin' Up Strangers'. I introduced him, and he said, "Dad, this is the biggest crowd I've ever played for in my life."

Johnny had his own band as well, and they were a good group. They used to practice in my garage. They called themselves 'Just Push Play'. They wrote some songs, and I sent those to myself by registered mail. This is called a 'Poor Man's Copyright'. It gives you a legal record of when you wrote a song, so someone else can't claim that they wrote it.

When I was away on tour, JL would have friends over. He was a master of cleaning up the house when he knew I was only ten minutes away.

JL was something else. He could have been anything he wanted to be. He had so much potential. But he was still trying to find himself. He got his associates degree from a technical college.

Johnny was so bright, so intelligent, and so funny. He was a great golfer, and he might have ended up being a professional golfer.

CHAPTER SIXTEEN

Losing Johnny

My son was my life.

And I never dreamed I would lose my son to drugs.

He started out with pain pills. They were the exact same thing that ended up taking his mother's life. My sister Jan asked JL, "Why in God's name would you start taking those pills when you knew that they killed your mom?"

JL looked at her and said, "I wanted to experience what she did. I wanted to see if I could understand how she could care more about those pills than she did me."

And boy, did he experience the same thing. He found out what she went through. And he gave his life to find out.

I was in such a state of denial with JL. I just didn't want to believe that my son was doing drugs. He got involved with the wrong people. He took heroin for the first time, and that is all it took. In an instant, the heroin took over my son. I watched him sink further and further into his addiction, but I still refused to see what was happening.

Cherish decided to move to Branson to live with us. She was going to be in JL's band, and she hadn't seen us in quite a while.

But the moment that JL picked her up at the airport, she knew that something was different about her brother.

As they talked, she quickly suspected he was on some kind of drug. It took her less than ten minutes to know that he wasn't right. I had lived with him every day and I could not see it! I was just not prepared, and I didn't want to see that my son had a problem.

When Cherish found out how bad Johnny was, she went out to our garage to call me. When I answered, she said, "Hey, we have a big problem on our hands."

Just as she said "Your son is a druggie," JL walked in on her. He started yelling at her, "What in the hell are you doing?! You are ratting me out to dad?!"

At that point, he was doing oxycontin. He was also doing heroin.

He didn't like what was happening to himself, but he couldn't stop it.

I thought that I could tell him to stop, and he would stop. But it was not that easy.

One time, while I was away, Johnny fell asleep in my bed, and while he was sleeping, Cherish went through all of his stuff. She found needles and all kinds of drugs. She called me and cried, "You need to come home now."

When JL woke up, Cherish told him, "Johnny, I found everything."

He finally admitted that he had a problem, and he told her that he had been shooting heroin.

When I got home, I was so pissed. I started screaming. I'm sure Cherish and Johnny thought I was going to kill both of them.

I was in the kitchen, and I took a big, heavy pan and slammed it against the counter. "What the hell is wrong with you?! Shooting heroin?!" I screamed at Johnny. "Are you crazy?!" I hit the pan so hard that it folded in half.

I wish I had known how addictive that drug was. One thing that I really regret is that I got so angry at him.

We sent Johnny to a halfway house, but he should have gone to rehab.

When she went through all of his stuff, Cherish had found the names, numbers and addresses of all of his drug dealers. She called the police and wanted to give them all to them, but the police refused to do anything.

Cherish did everything she could to get him to stop shooting heroin. One time, she talked him into drinking a bottle of vodka with her. She figured getting drunk was safer than shooting heroin.

The next day, Cherish asked to see JL's latest tattoo. He held out his arm to show a tattoo of our family tree, but when Cherish felt his forearm, it was hard as a rock. It was nothing but scar tissue from where he had been shooting heroin. Cherish started crying, "Oh, please don't do this to yourself!" Johnny started crying too, and they hugged each other.

Then things began to get worse. To pay for his drug habit, Johnny started stealing. He stole things from Cherish, and he stole from me. It started with just one or two small items every now and then, but then he ended up stealing so much.

He stole my guitars, my jewelry, and of course, any money I had in the house. He even ended up stealing our silverware. One day, I couldn't find one spoon in the kitchen!

JL had always been such a sweetheart, but those drugs make people do things they would never have done otherwise. Little by little, my house just kept getting emptier and emptier.

I finally had enough, and I called the police. I told them I had been robbed and that I knew who did it. I turned my son in. By that time, he had stolen more than $40,000 worth of musical instruments and jewelry.

But my love and support for my son never stopped. His half-sister also continued to support him. During the half year that he was in jail, Cherish talked to Johnny on the phone almost every day. They prayed together. Cherish had reconnected with her faith, and she shared that faith with Johnny.

JL was sentenced to six months in jail. During that time, I decided to move us out of Branson, to get him away from the people who were selling him drugs.

I wanted to get him the hell away from the scumbag drug dealers he was hanging around.

My plan was to let JL finish school at Texas A&M. He already had his associate's degree. I bought a beautiful ranch in Texas so that we all could have a brand new start.

Cherish loved the ranch, and I did too. It was 150 acres of paradise. And we waited for JL to get there. I had a guest house on the ranch for

Johnny. I had him a job. I was going to get his probation transferred down to Texas. I was going to change his life. I was going to save his life.

But Johnny never got to see that ranch.

I had arranged for him to have his parole transferred to Texas. Our plan was as soon as he was released from jail, he would get the hell out of Branson and down to his new life in Texas.

But the justice system really failed my son.

As he walked out of jail, they said, "You can't leave town. You have to check in with your parole agent here in Branson in two days."

After those two days, they said "You need to go here in two days." They kept jacking him around. I knew that if he stayed in Branson, he was a ticking time bomb. He had been completely clean and off drugs for six months, but since he couldn't get out of town, guess what happened? He found his drug dealing friend. And he did heroin one more time. Since his system had been clean, it wasn't used to the amount that he shot up, and he died.

If I knew who sold him the drugs, it wouldn't be good. It would not be good. The only reason that drug dealer is still walking this earth is that I didn't find out his name. If I had gotten his name, I would not have cared about the consequences. I wouldn't have cared! I would have had no problem walking up to that piece of scum and taking him out of this world.

A few days after Johnny died, I called the parole people. I don't remember my exact words to them, but I wasn't very pleasant. I told them that I hoped they got their heads out of their asses before they lost someone else's son.

Johnny Lee II passed away on April 18, 2014. He was only 23 years old.

Sometimes I can talk about it, and sometimes I can't. It is something that I am still not over. And I usually cry when I talk about Johnny.

I was in Shreveport, Louisiana when I got the call that my son was dead.

I had a show scheduled for that night. They would have understood if I canceled my concert that night, but I felt like I had to do the show. And I did it. It was one of the hardest things that I have ever had to do. My band and the club owner couldn't believe I did the concert. I was in a daze. But I got through it. I didn't drink anything before I went on. I knew that I had to keep my wits about me. I might have lost it if I had drank anything. Lord knows I felt like drinking.

My daughter Cherish remembers more about that night than I do.

> "I was in California when I got word that JL had died. I immediately flew to Louisiana where dad was playing that night.
>
> I walked onto his bus, and it was completely quiet. Dad was the only one on the bus. I just hugged him and held his hand. We held hands and cried until the time he walked on stage to do his show. He had made a commitment to do the concert, and it was right then that I finally understood my father. I thought, 'This is who he is. This is what he does. This is his life.' I sat on the side of the stage and watched him perform.
>
> After the show, we got in his car and drove back to his ranch. We held hands all the way. The next morning, we went home to Branson to start planning my brother's funeral."
>
> - Cherish Lee

I just wish there was something I could have done. I regret that I wasn't more educated about drugs when he got hooked. Maybe I could have done something different. The one thing I did learn is that no one can quit unless they really want to. It doesn't matter how many times they go to rehab; until they get it in their mind that they really want to quit, it ain't going to happen. God, I wish I could have done something different.

Even now, some days are just unbearable. A parent never expects to bury a child. It should be the other way around. We should go first. I have had to bury two children.

I stayed in Texas for a while after my son's death. But since he is buried in Branson, Missouri, I moved back there. I am comforted in knowing that I can go visit him, and I go to the cemetery quite often.

I will be driving around town, doing my errands, and I'll get the urge to go out to the cemetery to be with my son. I know that I can be close to him anytime I want to. It comforts me to go there to talk to my son and to pray.

At the cemetery, there is only one place where there are two plots left. When it's my time, I'm going to have him moved so that we will be side by side.

JL loved penguins, and I put flowers and stuffed penguins on his grave. I've got big bags full of stuffed penguins. I keep them in the garage. I buy those when I'm on the road, and every time I go to his grave, I put a new penguin there.

After his death, I got pretty heavy into the Jack Daniels. I didn't give a shit. I didn't care about anything.

But I finally came out of it. I knew my son wouldn't have wanted his death to ruin me.

Don't get me wrong, I can still throw down some Grey Goose vodka or Jack Daniels. But I like to be in control. If I'm going to get drunk, it will be after the show and on my bus.

When I sent my son away to try and get well, he made me promise that I would take care of his dog. Her name is Zoey. She turned into the best dog in the world.

I promised my son I'd take care of her, and I will continue to keep that promise for as long as Zoey lives. She is a living connection to my son. I also have a tattoo of her and Johnny on my arm.

I had a psychic reading done once with a famous medium, and he told me stuff about my son that really blew my mind. I had never met the guy before, but he knew things. He knew about Zoey, my son's dog. He knew about JL's death, and how he died. He told me that my son was with me. He said "Your son is shaking his head because you got those tattoos." The medium had never seen my tattoos! No one had. I'd like to think there is something to that.

I miss Johnny so much. There is not a second of the day that goes by that I don't wish I could see and touch him. I look forward to going to sleep at night, so that maybe he can come to me in a dream.

I can still hear him say "I Love you Dad." It is so loud and clear. Every day, I always pray for him. I talk to God, and ask him to bless his soul and keep his arms around him until I can be with him.

What do you do when your son is gone, but his car is sitting in your driveway? My sister Jan wants to tell you the answer.

> "Johnny bought his son a new car. It was a 2007 BMW 3 Series, 6 speed. JL loved that car!
>
> A short time after JL died, Johnny came in and said, 'I paid off JL's car.' Then he threw me the keys and said, 'Here ya go. It's yours.' I just lost it. I started crying right there. It meant a lot to me, because it was JL's car. It meant a lot that Johnny would trust me with the car, and that he wanted me to have it. But to think that he paid it off first so that I wouldn't have any bill… wow, that was amazing.
>
> I haven't taken anything out of the car. It is just like JL left it. It still has his change in the cup holder. His belt is still in there. The car has 'JL II' on the license plate. It means so much to me."
>
> - Jan Cerny, Johnny's sister

I never knew how loved Johnny was by so many of his friends. I found out after he passed away, when they posted on his Facebook page. Here are a couple of those posts:

> "I'm missing my best friend more than I can put into words. It has hit me hard. No matter how depressed, stressed or weary I was, I could always cope knowing my best friend was there. I wanted nothing more than to grow old with him. We shared so many emotional ups and downs together.
>
> I never thought I'd be able to carry on without him. He was truly my rock. A constant pillow of comfort, a pillar of strength, a lighthouse of hope that I could gravitate to. In the grand cosmic scheme of time, our existence is just a blink of an eye. With that said, cherish the ones you love.
>
> Death is real and it does not discriminate. Love the ones you

> hold close to heart. I know my brotha is a dimension away and I will meet him again way sooner than I can humanly conceive. I love and miss you Johnny. Always remember.
>
> Taylor Newsom

> "It's been over 6 months now, but it seems like yesterday.
>
> Truly one of the most devastating moments of my life and it happened without any warning. Disbelief, anguish and soul crushing sorrow. I can't physically put words to the emotion that overwhelmed me the day that I found out.
>
> I lost a brother. Only by grace was I able to hang on to the memories I had of our time together.
>
> The last time I saw you, we sat outside for half an hour and talked about all the good times. We talked about future and laughed just as hard as when we were 16. I still dream about that night, and in my dreams, I get to laugh with you one more time.
>
> I can never forget the joy you brought to my life. I'll love you forever Johnny.
>
> Jeremiah Grady

Any time you see me now, on stage or off, you will see that I am wearing a black, rubber bracelet. It says 'Always Remember', and I think of Johnny every time I look at that bracelet.

I never dreamed I would lose my son to drugs.

He was such an amazing person. And the drugs took his life way.

I miss him every time I blink my eyes. I miss him with every breath I take. There is not a moment that goes by in which he is not on my mind and in my heart.

Johnny was the love of my life. His headstone says 'He was my life. He was my love. He was my son.'

CHAPTER SEVENTEEN

Connor

What I am about to tell you will come as a shock to a lot of people.

But Johnny was not my only boy.

I have another son. His name is Connor.

As I write this, Connor Lee is 14 years old.

He came along shortly after I hired a pretty, blonde-haired bass player. Her name was Kelly. She was in my band.

When Kelly told me she was pregnant, I knew she wanted me to marry her. But I also knew that it just would not have worked out. It would have been a mistake, and we would have ended up divorcing, and I didn't want that for her or for me.

But she had Connor. I always paid her child support. I paid her a lot. But it seemed that we were always fighting over money. She seemed to always need more. So I didn't really go around them very much, when Connor was young.

Of course, my dad left me even before I was born. He was never there for me. And I hated him for that.

I do not want to be like my dad was. I want to be there for Connor.

Connor is a good boy. He looks a lot like me. And he is a lot like me.

He also lives in Branson, and he comes over and spends time with me as often as he can. My schedule doesn't make it very easy. When he is home from school on the weekend, we are usually gone.

I like to joke and laugh with Connor. He hugs me and we have long talks. We have a good time together.

I have gone to some of his school functions and activities, and I get along fine with his mother now.

I love Connor, and I would like to have a closer relationship with him. But I have not allowed myself to become as close to him as I did to JL. I don't know why that is. I don't know exactly what I am afraid of. I don't know if it is because I am afraid of losing him, or what. But I know that I am terrified to open myself up to Connor. I know that I have put up a barrier. I need to let my guard down, and I hope that sometime in the future, we can be a lot closer. It is a work in progress.

But I also know this… I will try to make a difference in his life. And I will be there if he ever needs me.

CHAPTER EIGHTEEN

Your Toupee Really sucks

I have lots of stories. All of these are true, too! And a lot of them are funny. Most of them are interesting, but they don't really have anything to do with anything else, so I've put them all together in this chapter.

My buddy Joe Ladd was one of the main disk jockeys in Houston, Texas, and he used to come out to Gilley's all the time. Joe had thinning hair, so he had gotten a hairpiece, and you couldn't tell that it wasn't his real hair.

He kept telling me I should get a hairpiece, so I saved up enough money and I got one. But since I wore a cowboy hat a lot, when I wasn't wearing the toupee, I would put in my car glove box, or in the passenger seat. But one night, for some reason, I put it under the driver's seat… and I forgot that it was there.

I had a big old Lincoln Continental, and I pulled into a car wash. It was a full service place, and as soon as you got out of your car, a bunch of Mexicans would start cleaning every inch of it. I was standing near the vehicle, as I watched one guy take the vacuum into the car. Just a second later, I heard "Swooooop!" He had sucked up my expensive hairpiece into his vacuum!

I was too embarrassed to tell them what had happened.

I drove away thinking, "I have now lost my hair twice." I never wore a toupee again.

Wearing a wig is also too much of a hassle. And I didn't want to be fake. I have always been myself. I tried to teach my kids that they need to be themselves. We need to be proud of who we are. So I didn't feel right when I was wearing a toupee, because I felt like I was trying to be someone I was not.

And besides, guys with a lot of hair will never know how good it feels to get kissed on the bald spot or get their head rubbed by a beautiful woman!

I was once elk hunting in Sargents, Colorado. Sargents is a tiny town. There are only about 50 people there. And they have a restaurant, a gas station, a bar and a store, all inside the same building. That's all there is.

I was sitting in the restaurant, and there was a beautiful waitress there. Of course, I hit on her. We didn't do anything that night, but I made plans to come back to see her.

I came back the next night, but she wasn't there. There was another cute girl there, though. So I put a move on her. I was sitting with my hunting buddies, and I asked them, "This is a small town. Do you think if I hook up with this woman tonight, the girl from last night will find out?" They said, "Probably so. That's her mother!"
Neither one of them panned out.

Every year, we play in La Marque, Texas. This past July 3rd, they announced that from now on, every July 3rd will be known as Johnny Lee Day in La Marque. That's a great honor.

La Marque is about 30 miles from where I was raised, so all of my old friends, classmates and family members always come and see us there.

My bus was parked behind the stage. My mom was on the bus. She put her walker at the bus door. My step uncle had a walker as well, and he put it by my mom's. My sister had just had surgery, and she had a walker. And one of my mother's friends had a walker! They had them all lined up at my bus door.

I had just got done signing autographs. I had been meeting so many pretty young ladies. I got to my bus and saw the walkers, and I said, "Whose walkers are these?! Get these things out of here! How do you expect me to get laid with all these walkers lined up at my bus! It looks I'm playing at an old folks home."

I have been able to meet and perform for quite a few U.S. Presidents. That's always an honor.

Jimmy Carter was a real cool guy. I met President Carter quite a few times. He loved country music, and was a big fan of mine.

I was invited to the White House to play for Ronald Reagan's inauguration. Me, Jerry Lee Lewis, and Kool and the Gang played the show. That was quite a combination!

The next day, they had a reception at the White House. Since it was such a formal occasion, I had to check my cowboy hat when I went in. When I walked in without it, hardly anyone recognized me! And my big ole belt buckle also set off the metal detector.

President Reagan was really nice to me. I also met Nancy Reagan. George Bush was Vice President. I said "Hello" to him and his wife Barbara.

And I got to visit with George Bush again, after he became President. He was also very nice, and was a huge country music fan.

During my time at the inauguration, I had a great time visiting the Lincoln and Jefferson Memorials. It was a real honor to be in Washington, D.C. during that historic time.

And President Gerald Ford played a joke on me.

We were at a golf tournament in Colorado, and that night, President Ford invited us to his house. I walked in, and he asked if he could make me a drink. I thought, "The President of the United States is going to fix me a drink? Wow!"

As we visited, I told him, "Mr. Ford, it ain't every day that an old country boy like me has the President of the United States to make him a drink. Can I please have this glass to take home?"

He whispered back to me, "Yes, you can take it, but don't tell Betty. It's part of a set, and she'll get pissed off!"

When I left, I put the glass inside my jacket. When I stepped outside, two secret service men grabbed me, reached into my jacket and took the glass. They said, "We need to arrest you for pilfering the President's home." I almost crapped my pants! But when I looked back, President Ford was laughing. As a joke, he had told his secret service guys to arrest me.

Phil Harris was a great comedian, jazz musician and singer. He made it big in the early days of radio, and he once told me, "Johnny, I knew I was getting old when I bent down to take off my alligator shoes… and I was barefooted."

I was playing in Phil's golf tournament in Linton, Indiana. An optometrist, Dr. Stewart picked me up at the airport. And he got lost driving me to the event. We saw an old man sitting on a porch, and we pulled over. The man was smoking a pipe, and I asked the man, "Can you tell me how to get to the Phil Harris Golf Course?"

He looked at me and said, "Well, are you walkin' or are you drivin'?"

I said, "Well, we're driving."

"That would be your quickest way," he said.

I was sitting on my bus in Crawford, Texas. Crawford is the home of President George W. Bush. My bus driver yelled back at me, "Boss, there are a bunch of girls out here!"

I said, "Hell, let 'em on the damn bus!"

He opened the bus door, and all these little girls started running onto the bus! It was the entire 6th grade class from Crawford Elementary School! Those little girls knew all the words to my songs. I introduced myself to every little girl. I had them laughing. I asked them if they were married, and where they worked at.

It did my heart so good to see all those girls giggling. We had a great visit. I ended up getting them up on stage with me to sing 'Lookin' for Love' at the concert that night. You can see a photo of all of us on my bus in the photo section.

I was in Mississippi when I pulled into a Subway sandwich shop. There was a real nice black lady working there. I ordered a sandwich and a diet Coke, and the woman said, "Don't you want the full meal deal?"

I asked, "What do I get if I get the full meal deal?"

"You get fuller," she said.

On September 3, 1983, I was honored to be adopted as a blood brother into the Kiowa Indian Tribe. My given Kiowa name is Ghotetsa. That means 'Strong Horse'.

Later, I was also adopted into the Culeo Patanegra Tribe. My given name is 'Walking Eagle'. That means... I'm too full of shit to fly!

I was playing at Gilley's in the summer of 1979. A woman used to come to the club on a regular basis, whose name was Margo Alexander. Margo was a quiet, shy girl. We became friends.

Margo asked me if she could paint a picture of Gilley's, and I said "Sure." Her painting shows Mickey with a beard, which he had at the time, and she also includes the people in the audience who came out to see us play every night.

When she had finished the painting, she brought it to Gilley's and gave it to me. On the way home that night, she was killed in a car accident.

I still have her painting hanging on the wall of my office. I treasure it. You can see a picture of it in the photo section.

Mickey and I were flying high, literally, in our King Air plane. Mickey was co-piloting the plane. The King Air was pressurized, and sometimes if some of the band had been drinking and were being a little too rowdy, Mickey would cut the oxygen back in the plane's cabin to make them fall asleep.

One time, our drummer Mike Schillaci had fallen into a deep sleep. So I took a Sharpie and drew bugs all over his face. Then, I colored half of his face red and the other half black. Gilley said, "Don't do his nose. His nose is so big that he will see it when he wakes up."

When Mike came to, no one said anything, but we couldn't help smiling as he walked off the plane. In the airport, we could see people looking at Mike's face, and quite a few laughed. But he had no idea what they were laughing at, until he went to the bathroom. When he looked into the mirror, he got angry. He was mad. And he continued to fume as we got back onto the plane. When we got up in the air, Mike started screaming at everyone, especially me. Mickey was trying to fly the plane, and he had this distraction in the form of an irate country music drummer.

Gilley turned around and yelled, "Mike, shut the hell up!"

But we meant no harm to Mike. We were just trying to pass the time. Every now and then, I would take a marker and draw bugs on the bedsheet of a band member's bunk or hotel room bed. They would crawl into bed, turn the sheet down, and see bugs all over their bed!

Mike Schillaci was able to get me back for my practical joking. He was always telling me it wasn't fair that I made all the big money and that the band members didn't get paid that much.

He also wore a pair of cowboy boots that had big holes in the soles of them. One night, we were in the dressing room, and a local DJ walked up to Mike and asked, "Who are you?"

Mike said, "I'm Mike. I work for Johnny Lee." Right at that moment, he leaned back, put his feet up on the table, and crossed his legs. The DJ looked at Mike's boots with the holes in the bottom. Mike said, "Yep, I work for Johnny Lee and Mickey Gilley.

I love the men and women of the U.S. military. When I did my Christmas CD 'Santa Claus is Lookin' for Love', it was back when the Iraq War had just started. My CD has a song on it called 'Red, White and Blue Christmas'. I signed 1,000 copies and gave them to soldiers who were headed to Iraq. I love our veterans, and I love those who are serving today.

We did quite a few shows with a local group called 'Mike and the Moonpies', and for some reason, during their sound checks they always played 'Cherokee Fiddle'. They did that at every show we did with them. There is kind of an unwritten rule that an opening act doesn't play the headliner's songs.

Johnnie Helms finally went up to them and said, "Guys, we appreciate you liking Johnny's song, but we ask that you not play it anymore during your sound check."

They said, "Sure, no problem." At the next show, during their sound check, they played "Lookin' for Love"!

I looked at Johnnie and said, "Let them do it. That's funnier than hell."

I ended up becoming friends with all of 'Mike and the Moonpies'. They are great guys.

I was in a piano bar with my good friend Omar. It was so loud in the bar that you kind of had to read people's lips.

This beautiful girl came up to Omar and asked, "Are you married?" He said, "Hell no!" Well, Omar's wife was standing right behind him. She tapped him on the shoulder and said, "Excuse me? You say you are not married?"

Omar yelled, "Of course I am! I thought she asked 'Are you Larry?'"

I met Edwin McCain at John Daly's golf tournament. He toured with Hootie and the Blowfish, and had a huge hit with 'I'll Be'.

Edwin became a great friend. He was adopted when he was a little boy. And after we'd gotten to know each other, he started telling people as a joke that I was his real dad.

We were doing a show together in Illinois, and Edwin did an interview with a newspaper reporter. Then, when he jokingly said that I was his dad, the reporter believed him and put it in the paper!

That night at the concert, Edwin told the crowd, "Tonight I am going to reveal who my real father is." He had a big yellow envelope that said 'DNA' on it. As he opened it, our drummer gave him a big drumroll. Edwin looked at me as he read, "And my real daddy is… Meat Loaf!"

3 Things You Didn't Know About Johnny Lee

1. Favorite TV show: The Price is Right
2. Favorite TV Network: QVC
3. He keeps his home spotless, and his bed sheets smell like perfume

My favorite TV show is 'The Price is Right'. Don't be calling me when 'The Price is Right' is on! I even got Mickey Gilley hooked on the show. If you call Mickey's answering machine, you will get a message that says, "This is Gilley. If you called me at 10:00, I am watching 'The Price is Right'. If you called me at 2:00, I'm probably taking a nap."

I love 'The Price is Right'. I almost went into withdrawals when Bob Barker quit the show. When Drew Carrey came on, I thought 'This is not going to work,' but he ended up being perfect for the show.

I love the action of the big wheel. I get pissed off when the people don't have a clue of what the prices of the things are.

I also watch a lot of QVC. I buy a lot of things off of there. Some of the best steaks that I have ever had in my life were ones that I bought on QVC. I buy those big filets. They come from the Kansas City Meat Company. I also like to get Junior's Cheesecake.

But I have found that QVC and Grey Goose do not mix. I would watch QVC when I was drunk, and a few days later, the packages would start piling up at my door! I had no idea what all I had even bought.

I love QVC. I was actually on there a couple of times, selling 'Gilley's Greatest Hits'. Their hosts are so rehearsed, and they always know what's coming next... until I came on! We started taking calls, and one guy started asking about my sister. Right on the air, I told him, "You can probably find my sister's number on any men's room wall in New Orleans." The QVC host about fell over!

I also like 'Dancing with the Stars'. I like all the beautiful women on there. And I watch a lot of the 'Food Network' too. I like to cook, and I learn a lot from that channel.

I like things that smell nice. I like my bedsheets to smell nice, and I found this detergent called Diva... it's from a candle company. It costs about a hundred dollars a jug, but if you wash your sheets with it and then spray your bed with some 'Midnight Romance' perfume, it will make you want to eat your damn pillows! I sent a jug of the Diva detergent to my daughter. Her mom, Charlene, didn't know how expensive it was, and she washed some dog towels with it. Cherish smelled those dog towels, and she hid the detergent from her mom!

I have a thing about clean, fresh sheets. That's one of the things I look forward to when I come home from off the road. I want to get in my clean, fresh and wonderful-smelling bed.

I like a very clean house.

When I was a kid growing up in Alta Loma, when we turned the lights on in our little house, we could see the roaches running around. I hated that.

When I went into the military, I really appreciated it when they made everyone be neat and clean. They thought that they were punishing us. It would have probably made them mad to know that I really liked making my bed, and making sure that me and my clothes were in perfect condition!

I have it in my concert contracts that we only stay in nice hotels. We don't stay in crappy places.

I also keep my bus clean, and I always change the bus air filters so that our circulating air is as clean as possible. I tell my band members, "If you see dust on the bus, wipe it down. We don't want to breathe bad, dirty air." I do not allow smoking on the bus. And the number one bus rule? No number two on the bus! That's why they invented truck stops.

CHAPTER NINETEEN

Entertaining

"If you want to make a livin', you gotta put on a good show."

I always said that I would be successful in this business… or I would die trying. And if I died trying, at least I would have been working toward my goal.

I say a prayer before each concert that I do.

I thank God for my talent. I thank him for the opportunity that I have that night, and I ask him to help me do a good job. Sometimes, I'll dedicate the show to my son. Sometimes, I dedicate it to my Uncle Jimmy. He was the one who always told everyone that I was a great singer. And I just ask God to help me to be successful.

When I do a show with other artists, I can go on first, second, third or fourth. I don't care where I go on in a show. I can open a concert, and I can close the show.

I never warm up my voice before a concert. I just go out and sing. I've never taken a voice lesson.

I never have a set song list, either. Most artists put a list of their songs on a sheet of paper, and set it on the floor in front of them on the stage. If I gave my band a set list, they would laugh at me. I do my show by feel. I need to feel what the crowd is wanting. I can tell if they need a fast, happy song, or if they want a slow, sad love song.

I have a little thing that I do when I am doing a concert…

After my first song or two, as the people applaud, I will say, "No, no, no. Stop. Please no more." But at the same time, I am gesturing with my hands for them to keep their cheering and applause coming!

It really sounds good when I'm on the Opry and it is being broadcasted on the radio. All the radio listeners can hear is me saying,

"Please, no more." They can't see my hands asking for more applause on the radio!

It becomes funny to the audience. Then sometimes, when they stop clapping, I'll say, "Is that it?"

Every now and then, a woman will yell out and I'll say, "Thank you ma'am. It's been a long time since I made a lady scream."

During the show, I like to come off the stage and get down in the crowd. But when I do that now, I always wonder how I'm going to get back up on stage. My ankles are messed up, and I can't jump as high as I used to. It's like that old joke... I can jump as high, but I can't stay up as long as I used to.

I like to be funny. I like to make people laugh and put a smile on their face. I can't go on stage and just sing my songs, I need to entertain my fans. I'm a people person.

There is nothing better to me than doing a great show. That's who I am. That's what I'm all about. And when I get a standing ovation, it is so satisfying.

I'm very blessed and fortunate, and I'm thankful for all of my fans. I've been very lucky. I've worked hard for it, though.

After my show is over, I will sit and sign every autograph and take each picture until every single person gets one. To me, meeting all the fans after the show is as important as the actual show.

I always loved Fan Fair in Nashville. I would sit in the booth all day. I'd meet everybody, and I'd take pictures and sign autographs. I would be so exhausted at the end of the day. Mickey Gilley and I would meet so many people. We were glad to see everybody. We didn't use bodyguards; we wanted the fans to get close to us. Hell, I even got a few dates from there!

Mickey told me, "Always take care of your fans." To this day, I'm always the last one to leave the building. I love to make people happy.

As I mentioned, I love to make people laugh, and there is one story that I have told that people remember more than all the others.

During one of Larry Black's 'Country's Family Reunion' TV shows, I told this story that has followed me ever since…

We used to have breakfast with Mickey Gilley's parents. We'd go to their home, and Mickey's mom would make the best biscuits in the world.

Most people know that Mickey has two famous cousins, Reverend Jimmy Swaggart and Jerry Lee Lewis. Of course, Jerry is a rock n roll legend. And Mickey, Jimmy and Jerry are all first cousins.

One morning, they were all at Mickey's parents' when we came over for breakfast.

The Gilley's were country folks. But they were 'Up-town' country folks. They were so country that they had an outhouse for a bathroom, but they were 'Up-town', because they had a fancy three-holer. A three-holer is an outhouse that has three holes that you can use. Most folks just had one hole.

We were all sitting at the table, having breakfast, and we were really enjoying those great biscuits Mrs. Gilley made. And Jerry Lee excused himself to go to the bathroom.

A couple minutes later he came running in, asking for a coat hanger. He unwound the hanger and ran back to the outhouse. I followed him, and he took that hanger and put it down the center hole. I said, "Killer, what are you doing?"

He said, "My coat fell down this hole."

"You ain't going to wear that thing, are you?!" I exclaimed.

He said, "No, but I've got a biscuit in the pocket!"

Anytime I am out, almost every day someone will come up to me and say, "Hey, is that a biscuit in your pocket?!"

I say, "No, I'm just glad to see you."

I went on the 'Country's Family Reunion' cruise, and I got a bunch of biscuits from the buffet. I let them get hard, and then I signed them. And during my show, I threw them out to the crowd. All these old people were fighting over those biscuits!

I met a woman on that cruise. She had big diamond rings and gold necklaces on, and she had a big, beehive hair-do that I know had a can of Aqua-net hair spray on it. She came up to me and said, "Johnny Lee! You look exactly like my sixth husband!"

I said, "Sixth?! How many times have you been married?"

She said, "Five."

I said, "Bye, bye."

CHAPTER TWENTY

Fore!

I'm too old to play football. I refuse to chase a tennis ball around. My knees and my ankles couldn't handle a tennis court. And the last time I played in a celebrity softball game, Wade Boggs said that clocked me with a sun dial.

Thank God for golf.

I love golf.

The first time I ever held a golf club I was at Montgomery Wards on Spencer Highway in Pasadena Texas. I was in the sporting goods department when a guy came in to sell golf clubs. He brought in a big TV monitor that he used to show how you held your clubs. But I was more interested in just seeing myself on that TV!

He showed me how to use an interlocking grip. I still use it to this day. He taught me how to swing and he'd show it back to me on the television screen. But I knew I couldn't afford the clubs he was selling. Instead, I went to a pawn shop and got me some clubs. I also bought some cleats. I used to love to walk on those cleats. There was something about the cleats that made me feel cool.

I still remember my first round of golf. It was at the Glenbrook Golf Course in Houston, Texas. My pocket was bulging out with golf tees. I stuck a tee into the ground, put the ball on the tee, and hit it as hard as I could. Then I walked up to the ball, took a tee out from my pocket, put the ball on the tee and hit it again. As I got closer to the hole, I kept sticking a new tee into the ground and hitting the ball off of it.

When I finally got to the green, I thought that it might be easier to not put it on a tee and just putt it off the ground.

When we moved to the second hole and I started to get all my tees out again, my playing partner said, "What the hell are you doing?! You can't put the ball on the tee every shot!"

But practice makes perfect… at least, it makes you a lot better. And I got pretty good. I kept playing and playing. I couldn't afford to rent a golf cart so I'd carry that big golf bag and walk all 18 holes.

Mickey Gilley asked me how I spent my free time during the day. I said, "I play golf. You need to try it. You will either love it or you'll hate it."

I told Mickey that I would teach him how to golf and he agreed to meet me at Glenbrook. But Mickey didn't want to go to the driving range to practice, he just wanted to go play.

I knew we were starting from scratch. He didn't know anything about golf, so I told him, "This is called a tee. You stick it in the ground, put the ball on top of it, and hit the ball toward that flag down there." He said, "It'll be easy to hit that little ball with this big ole club. I'll knock it past that flag." I said, "Go ahead."

He swung as hard as he could and missed everything! He swung again, and missed. Then I showed him how to hold his club. When he finally did hit it, the ball went straight into the woods. He has been hooked on golf ever since.

Mickey started playing golf almost every day. And he ended up getting almost as good as me. I wasn't all that good, but we both had a lot of fun.

It's a wonder we didn't die on the course. When a thunderstorm would come in, we'd grab our clubs. I'd put my arms around the grips and hover over them so they wouldn't get wet. We'd stand under a tree to stay dry. We had no idea how stupid that was. We could have gotten killed by lightning.

Mickey Gilley used to 'mind fuck' me. Anyone who plays golf knows what that is. He used to really get under my skin. He would mess with me.

I used to get mad if Mickey was playing well and I wasn't. I'd throw a club and Mickey would laugh. But once I threw a club and it got stuck up in a tree. That made me madder. So I threw another club up at the one in the tree and that one also got hung up. Gilley started laughing. I got even madder so I threw my cap on the ground and stomped on it. Then I realized it was stuck to my golf cleats! I am much calmer on the course today.

I got Lasik eye surgery a few years ago. The main reason I got it was I wanted to be able to watch the flight of my golf ball. But I should have waited a few years. Now I don't hit the ball as far as I used to and I don't have to look so far down the golf course to see it!

I've played lots of golf in Hawaii. And I've had the honor of playing on some of the best golf courses around the world. I've played in England, Ireland and Japan. I love golf. I love it. It is something I will enjoy for the rest of my life.

I passed my love for golf on to my son. When he was just a little guy, I took him out to the golf course and taught him how to hit balls. JL was a natural talent. He could have been one of the greats.

And I've been able to golf with the greatest golfers in the world. I've played with Arnold Palmer, Jack Nicklaus, Chi Chi Rodriguez, Lee Trevino, Ben Crenshaw, Orville Moody, Meg Mallon, Helen Alfredsson, Nancy Lopez, Jan Stephenson, Natalie Gulbis, Val Skinner and Michelle Wie.

When I met Michelle Wie, for some reason, I thought she was from Japan. So I said to her phonetically, real slow, "I-brought-you-some-CDs." John Daly said, "You dumb ass. She went to the University of Hawaii!" She is better at English than I am. I was so embarrassed.

Orville Moody won the 1969 U.S. Open. The last time I played in a tournament with Orville, me and Ray Benson from the group Asleep at the Wheel won the Seniors Golf event. We got diamond rings for winning the tournament.

Doug Sanders is one of my dearest friends. I loved playing in Doug Sanders' Celebrity Classic. Doug had Presidents Gerald Ford, Jimmy Carter and George Bush play in his tournaments. I played with the Vice President Dan Quayle. He was really cool. I told him a few jokes and he really cracked up over them

I also got to golf with Evel Knievel. Evel liked to bet big money on all of his golf games. I always loved playing with my good friend Lee Elder. Lee was the first African American to play in the Masters Tournament. I even golfed with 'Mr. Cub' Ernie Banks.

I was playing with Jim McMahan. Jim was quarterback for the Chicago Bears. He had led the Bears to the World Championship and he was the hottest quarterback in the NFL at the time.

Jim and I were playing. I had a caddy. And Jim not only had a caddy, but he also had a guy who carried his cigars and his beer. Jim always played barefooted and he had a beer every hole. On about the fifth hole, I bowed out from drinking a beer. I knew if I was going to finish that tournament that I couldn't have a beer on each hole. To this day, I still love Jim McMahon. He is a great guy.

My country music friend Moe Bandy is one of my favorite golfing buddies. Our most memorable day on the course came during a round when Moe had managed to drive a ball right into my back. We were playing with Don Williams. Not Don Williams, the country singer; this Don is Andy Williams' brother. After I'd gotten my breath back from Moe's drive into my back, we drove a cart to the next hole.

But Moe somehow drove the cart off the path, and managed to get it stuck in mud. I got off, and started rocking the very heavy cart. Moe was behind the wheel, with his foot on the gas pedal. I was using all of my strength rocking the cart, and just as the back wheels got traction, Moe drove that cart at about 25 miles an hour… right over my foot! It left black tread marks on my new shoes.

As I limped to get back into the cart, I told him, "Moe, the next time I golf with you, I am going to suit up!"

"Johnny and I always have a great time when we are together.

Besides the times he has already mentioned, I remember one very interesting day on the golf course.

One day, I was driving the golf cart. We had stopped to look at some peach trees, when another cart ran right into the back of us. Johnny looked at me and I said, 'I didn't do it! I was just sitting here!'

Later, there were some older men ahead of us. They were really taking their time, and me and Johnny waited and waited. Finally, Johnny yelled, 'Get the hell out of the way!' It was so loud, you could have heard him two counties over.

Then as we got closer to them, Johnny yelled, 'You need to pick it up! You look like the movie "The Walking Dead"!' The old guys got mad, and when we finished our round, we got reprimanded by the

> clubhouse officials. Johnny didn't care."
>
> — Moe Bandy

I met John Daly at a golf tournament in Memphis. John was a big fan of mine, and I was a big fan of his.

He was hosting a tournament for the Make-A-Wish foundation, and they had a bunch of celebrities playing. The one that I remember the most was Irlene Mandrell. I used to have the hots for her real bad. At the show that night, Irlene was playing the drums, and then I got on the drums to play for Vince Gill. I just enjoyed sitting in the same seat where Irlene had been!

In 1983, I hosted the first annual Johnny Lee Pro Am Golf Tournament. We gave all the money that we raised to The Guiding Hands Foundation in California. That is a home for the mentally and physically handicapped.

I hosted that event for quite a few years, and we raised a lot of money. I invited John Daly to play in the tournament, and we really hit it off.

But I'm glad I met him when I did. If I'd have met him back during his crazier days, and back when I was really crazy, who knows what would have happened.

We were both pretty crazy when we started hanging around each other, but neither of us would probably be here if we had met ten years earlier.

One day, we were at John's house, when he decided that he wanted to go to a casino. John was doing some serious gambling back then, so serious that when he picked up the phone to call a casino in Louisiana, they immediately sent a private jet to pick us up.

As we left for the airport, it started storming really bad. There were tornado warnings and everything. But John said, "Come on, let's go."

By the time we got to the airport, I was hearing Buddy Holly music. I knew our little plane would crash in that storm. I was scared.

John drove his Hummer right out onto the runway to wait for our plane. When it arrived, the pilot taxied in, and rolled it right up to John's car. But that plane kept rolling, and the wing crashed into his car and knocked the windshield out.

The storm started getting even worse, and I refused to get on the plane. I finally talked John into going back home so that we could live to gamble another day.

"I met Johnny Lee in the early 1990s. He came to my golf tournament in Memphis. He ended up playing in my charity golf tournaments for 18 straight years.

I just loved his music. But I found that we got along so well. He was so funny. He is such a lovable guy, and we have a lot in common.

Johnny is basically my best friend.

We have been there for each other. We have supported each other through our many ups and downs. That's what best friends do.

The toughest thing in his life was the loss of his son, Johnny. That would be tough on anybody. It was a rough deal. I tried to help him through that.

I try to go to as many of his shows as I can. I like to surprise him, and pop up out of nowhere.

One of my favorite memories of Johnny is when he drove my bus. He was thinking about buying a new bus. I was traveling from Arkansas to California in my bus, and he went with me.

I drove the bus for a few hours, and then Johnny said, "I will drive for a little bit." But once he got in the driver's seat, he never got up. He drove that bus the whole way to California. He drove for at least 13 hours. Here he was, a big star. He could have been back in the 'star suite'. But he loved driving that bus.

We have had a lot of laughs together. Without a doubt, my most vivid memory of Johnny is of when he sat at the Head table at one of my golf tournaments. If he's got the guts, I think he will share that story… in the R-Rated chapter of this book.

We have stayed friends through all my troubles, and all of his troubles. We have helped each other through everything. That's what friendship is all about.

Johnny has always been there for me. I just love him. He is a like a brother to me."

- John Daly, 1991 PGA Champion

CHAPTER TWENTY ONE

Just The Good Ole Boys

I have many famous friends, but I also have many friends whom you have never heard of. My life has been made better because of these friends. Please know that there is no way that I could mention all of my friends and family members, but I know that even if they don't see their name here, they will still know that I love them very much.

Most of my friends are just good ole boys… and girls. They are regular people, from all walks of life, but they have one thing in common… they have all been a blessing to me.

Some of my best friends are cops, highway patrolmen and Texas Rangers.

One of my very best friends is named Snuffy. He is now a narcotics lieutenant in Texas. His real name is Roger Garrett. He got his name "Snuffy" when he was working in a penitentiary. He always had a dip of snuff in his mouth when he was there, and some of the convicts started calling him Snuffy.

He was working security at one of my shows, and he also drove me to and from the airport, and we just hit it off. But our friendship got off to an interesting start.

The first time I met Snuffy was at the airport in Austin Texas. I was playing at the Austin County Fair. I got off a small plane and was looking for my ride that was supposed to pick me up. I saw two policemen standing there. Snuffy was one of them.

They asked me, "Do you want a ride?" I said, "Not with you guys." I thought they were waiting on a prisoner or something. I walked outside and found that my ride wasn't there. So I walked back in the airport and those two cops asked me again, "Are you sure you don't want a ride?" Again, I said, "No, I'm waiting for the people from the fair to pick me up."

I waited about 15 minutes and the policemen came up and said,

"You probably need to come with us." Snuffy finally told me that they were the people I was waiting on. He just wanted to see how long it took me to get upset!

My family has a Christmas tradition: every year, we pick one person who we have met in the past year, and we call them to wish them a Merry Christmas. That year, I chose Snuffy. I could tell he was surprised when he answered, and I said, "Snuffy, you might not remember me, but this is Johnny Lee." And that was the start of one of the greatest friendships of my life.

Snuffy's dad was murdered. Before his death, his dad gave Snuffy five silver dollars, and told him, "If you can find someone who is a true friend, someone who would do anything in the world for you, someone who will stand by you through anything, I want you to give them one of these silver dollars. If you can find five people through your entire life to give the dollars to, then you will be a very fortunate person."

Snuffy ended up giving me one of those silver dollars. And I carry it with me everywhere I go. When he heard that I was writing this book, he said he had a few things he wanted to get off his chest…

"I have worked the stage security at our county fair for the last 25 years. Me and my friend Richard Holloman were asked to drive an hour and a half to pick up Johnny Lee.

Richard and I had both worked all night. About halfway into our hour and a half drive, Johnny said, 'You guys look tired. I can drive the rest of the way.' And he did! I moved to the passenger seat, while Richard got in the back, and the star of the show drove the car! I have worked with stars for over 20 years, and I have never met another person like Johnny.

If you call Johnny Lee in the morning, and you catch him in the middle of watching "The Price is Right", it will ruin his entire day. If he's hunting early in the morning, he's got to be back in before "The Price is Right" is on. He hollers at the people on the TV. He'll yell, 'No! No! No! It's 654 dollars! I know what recliners cost!' I'll look at him and say, 'Those people can't hear you.' His whole morning revolves around "The Price is Right"!

Johnny has one huge problem.

His heart is too big.

He would give the shirt off his back to someone he didn't even know.

I had a four month old grandbaby die. My grandson's funeral was held in a little church outside of Bellville, Texas. During the funeral, I looked up the aisle, and this guy wearing flip flops and sweat pants was walking in. It was Johnny Lee. He apologized for the way he was dressed. He said he would have missed his plane if he had changed clothes. I couldn't believe he had come all the way there.

And that wasn't the only trip to Texas Johnny made for my family. When my daughter Kimberly was getting married, he drove down and sang at her wedding and reception for free. He also wrote a special song for my daughter and I to dance to at her reception. He is a hell of a guy.

My favorite Johnny Lee song is 'Hey Bartender', and Johnny has already promised that he will sing it at my funeral. If I happen to outlive him, I already have it in my funeral plans that they will play a tape of 'Hey Bartender'.

If the world was full of Johnny Lees, it would be a much better place. He has such a good heart. I wish everyone could see that side of him. He is one of the best men I have ever met. I am fortunate to have him for a friend. His song 'One in a Million'… that is definitely Johnny."

— Snuffy Garrett

Snuffy also has another daughter, and her name is Jaclyn Duncan. But I never call her by her real name.

About 15 years ago, me and Snuffy were in his truck in Texas. Jaclyn met us, got in the truck, and I said, "What's that smell?"

She said, "It's my perfume. It's Estee Lauter, by God!" And from that moment on, I have called her "ES Day By God Lauder"! If I know she's coming to one of my shows, I will leave her tickets at the door, but she has to tell them she is ES Day By God Lauder!

When she heard about my book, ES Day… I mean Jaclyn, told me that she had a few things to say.

"I was a Vice President at a local bank, and on my birthday, every single year, Johnny would call me at the bank. He would ask whoever answered the phone to put him on the intercom system. Everyone would be doing their work, and all of a sudden, they heard this big voice coming through the speakers all around the building. He said, 'I want to wish ES Day By God Lauder a Happy Birthday! And I'm going to sing Happy Birthday to her right now!' And he did.

Every birthday, I knew I would get a call from him. One year, I was in the middle of a board of directors meeting. We were told that we couldn't take calls during the meeting, but all of a sudden, here came Johnny's voice booming over the intercom! All of the board members just sat there, completely speechless!

Most people think Johnny's tour bus is one big, rowdy party after his shows. I can tell you firsthand that that is not always the case.

He was singing at the Austin County Fair, and I was on the bus with my dad and my little boy, who was two years old at the time. When my little boy got tired, Johnny took him in the back and laid him in his big bed. Some other people were getting a little loud in the front of the bus, and Johnny loudly whispered to them, 'Hey, Hey! You all need to quiet down. The baby is sleeping back there.' He probably won't like me telling that, since it might ruin his wild and crazy and rowdy reputation.

There is no better man to be a part of your family through good times and through extra hard times.

The all-time hardest time came a few years ago. My husband died just one week before Johnny's son died. I didn't leave the house for almost a month. But Johnny called me, and said he was going back to performing and that his first show was going to be in Texas. He said, 'I want you to come see me. We need to start going on with our lives and we are going to start together.'

Other than my dad, Johnny is the number one man on this earth who I know that I can count on. My family has been so blessed to have him in our lives."

– Jaclyn (ES Day) Duncan

Gary Huitt lives in Virginia, and likes to send me anything from Chesapeake Bay. One time, he sent me four cases of live crabs. I had to clean every one of them. If you don't clean them just right, they can poison you, so I had to learn how to clean and freeze them all. But now he gives me ones that are already cleaned.

When I got my knee replaced, I went to stay with Gary. Gary and his wife took care of me as I healed up. He has done so much for me. He built my Camaro. He's just been a great friend. He's got a little dog named Chico, and Chico loves me as much as Gary does.

I met Bama when I moved to Branson. Bama's real name is Jackson Williams, but he got his nickname because he played football for coach Bear Bryant at the University of Alabama.

Bama has been a good buddy of mine for a long time. We drove from Branson to Denver together. We were passing through Kansas, and we saw a sign that said, "The original home of General Armstrong Custer".

I asked Bama, "I wonder which one of those homes belonged to Custer?"

Bama said, "The one with all the arrows and feathers sticking out of it!"

Larry Buxton is one of my best friends in the world. He used to be a bouncer at clubs in Louisiana. He started coming to Gilley's, and we became friends. He got into the oil business, and became very successful.

One night, he was going to a restaurant, and as he walked in, he tripped over a bush and broke his ankle. And before it was all over, he ended up losing his leg.

Every year, he takes me deer hunting in south Texas.

One year, we had bunk beds at our camp. He was sleeping on the top bunk, and in the middle of the night, he fell out of bed and landed right in his suitcase!

Steve Thomas is one of my best friends. I met him at a golf tournament in Tucson, Arizona. Dick Butkus, the famous Chicago Bear, was also there, and Steve, Dick and I all decided to go to a nearby country music bar.

When the band took a break, the lead singer walked by our table and asked, "Hey, are you Johnny Lee?"

I looked across the table at Steve and Dick, and said, "They even know me here, fellas."

Dick Butkus said, "Yeah, and that tour jacket you're wearing that has 'Johnny Lee' in huge letters on the back kind of gives them a hint!"

Me and Steve ended up on stage singing Elvis songs for a half hour, that night.

Steve and I have now been friends for over 20 years. We like to play practical jokes on each other.

One year, we were at a celebrity golf tournament, and we were at a table with Cheryl Ladd from Charlie's Angels, the comedian Pat Paulsen, and some other TV folks. When Steve went to the restroom, he left his glass of red wine on the table. I took the glass and covered it with see-through cellophane tape. When he sat back down at the table, he tried to sip the wine. He couldn't figure out why he wasn't getting any. Then, he tipped the glass so far back that it poured out all over his white shirt, his tie and his jacket.

But he got me back the next morning. We were all supposed to leave early, but I had met a pretty professional golfer. I wanted to spend some extra time with her, so I told everyone that I would take an afternoon flight so I could sleep in until noon.

Steve had to leave at 4:30 am, and as he passed the hotel lobby desk, he stopped and told them, "Johnny Lee wanted to sleep in a little longer, so can you please give a wakeup call at 5 am?"

The gal at the desk said, "Yes, I will call him right at 5:00 am."

I had been busy all night, and didn't get to sleep until about 4:00.

The hotel clerk called me an hour later! I was totally asleep when I reached over to get the phone, and I had an almost full bottle of beer on the stand next to me. When I reached for the phone, I knocked it over, and the whole bottle of beer poured out into one of my brand new cowboy boots!"

I met Rick Sutcliffe in 1980, when he was playing for the Los Angeles Dodgers. He had won the National League Rookie of the Year award in 1979, so he was pretty hot stuff at the time.

The Dodgers were playing a day game in Houston, and after the game that night, they all headed to Gilley's. Steve Howe, Bob Welch, Don Sutton and a lot of the other players all came in.

I went over to say hello to them, and Rick and I just became instant friends. We became so close that I would stay with him and his wife when I went to Los Angeles to film different TV shows. And our friendship continues today. When Rick heard I was doing this book, he asked if he could share a few memories...

"Urban Cowboy had just come out. Gilley's was absolutely packed and everyone was just going crazy over Johnny.

To me, meeting Johnny was like I was meeting Elvis Presley. He was so popular! Johnny was the first big musical star, and the most famous person, that I had ever met.

Johnny gave me one of the coolest gifts I have ever received. He showed up at Dodger stadium and gave me one of his Charlie 1 Horse hats. I think I slept in that hat for the first two years that I had it. I've got a framed picture of me and him wearing our hats.

I consider him one of my best friends on Earth, but I know there are probably 500 people who will tell you the same thing about Johnny. He is just a great friend to so many people.

Nine years ago, I was planning a charity golf tournament and concert. The proceeds were going to help build a children's hospital in

Lee Summit, Missouri. The tournament was in June, but five months earlier in February, I was diagnosed with colon cancer.

I went through chemo and radiation. I wore an ileostomy bag for eight months, and I didn't know if I was going to be able to hold the fundraiser. But Johnny called and said, 'We are going to put on that concert! And I am not missing that tournament.' He was really the reason that I went ahead with the tournament. He was also the reason that the concert sold out, and he wouldn't take a dime for doing the show. All the money we raised that day for the children's hospital would not have happened without Johnny Lee.

Johnny had already beaten his colon cancer, and when he found out about mine, he was a great friend and source for me. He shared what he went through, and things he would do different. He gave such encouragement that I was going to be OK. We were both lucky. We were both real lucky.

Johnny is so fun. There is never a dull moment with him. We have a friendship where we don't have to talk every day or see each other every week, but we just know that if there is anything either of us needs, we are there for each other.

He has also been a good influence on me, as I watched how he treated people. He never looked down at anyone, and he treated his fans so great. He never changed, no matter how successful he became. And I knew that I should be the same way and never change, no matter how much fame or fortune came my way.

When I walked into Gilley's that night, I had no clue that it would lead to a lifelong friendship with one of the greatest guys I have ever met.

– Rick Sutcliffe, The Red Baron

On stage with President Ford, his wife Betty, John Denver, Charley Pride, Floyd Cramer, Dinah Shore, Bob Hope, and Mickey. Im on the far right.

President Gerald Ford

Showing First Lady Betty Ford a photo of my daughter

Hanging out with Charlie Daniels

Onstage with Charlie Daniels

Three Lees...
Johnny Lee,
Brenda Lee, and
Jerry Lee Lewis

Singing
The Yellow Rose
with Lane Brody

With Lane Brody
Courtesy Judy Mock

Deb and I were married on November 14, 1986 in Maui, Hawaii.

Just after our wedding, I took Deb's mother and step father and my mom and Cherish on a cruise.

Out on the town with Debbie and Cherish

Deb and I visit with Gilligan's Island Skipper Alan Hale

President Carter loved Country Music

President Carter laughing at one of my jokes

What an honor it was to play at the inauguration of President Ronald Reagan

Meeting George and Barbara Bush. President Bush was a huge country music fan.

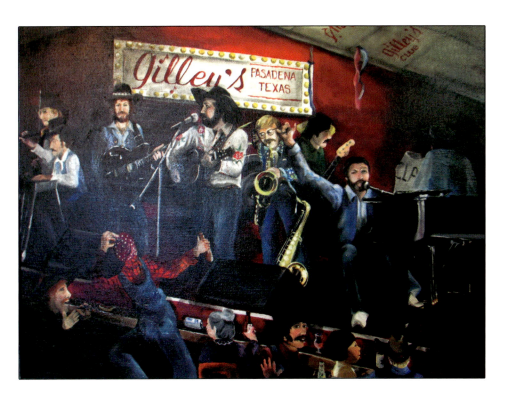

This painting by Margo Alexander hangs on my office wall. She gave it to me at Gilley's. She was killed in a car accident on her way home that night.

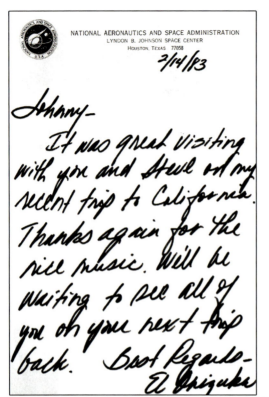

On Valentine's Day 1983, my friend El Onizuka wrote me this letter from the Johnson Space Center.

I treasure this photo signed by Ellison Onizuka. El died on the space shuttle Challenger.

The day I was adopted into the Kiowa Tribe

Getting my new name, Strong Horse. September 3, 1983

I asked Clyde the orangutan if he liked Mickey Gilley.
He gave Mickey the finger.

Updated photo of my family. (Left to right) Jimmy, Claudia, Me, Janet, Mom, Lynn, Janice

When Deb found out she was pregnant, I met her at the Tuscon Arizona airport dressed up as a baby!

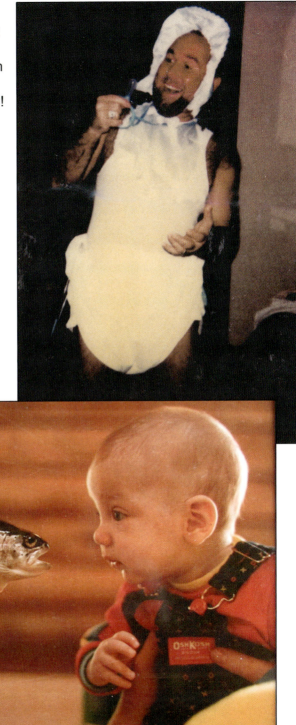

My son Johnny meets his first fish...up close and personal

My favorite photo with my son

The loves of my life, Johnny and Cherish, 1997

Johnny Lee the Second drumming during soundcheck

Proud papa with my son on stage

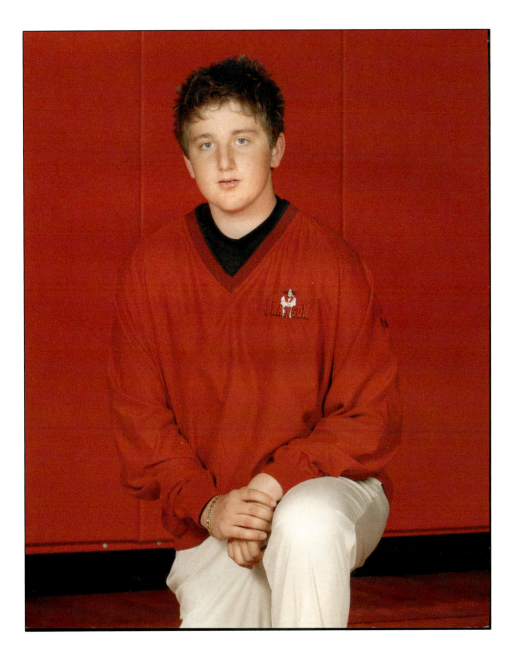

Johnny Lee the Second in Jr. High

Posing with Johnny

Johnny and his dog Zoey

18 holes with my friend John Daly

Golfing with Chicago Bear great Jim McMahan

My great friend Doug Sanders

Golfing with Dick Butkis

Another round with Dick Butkis and Steve Thomas

Clowning around with my pal Larry Buxton

John Daly helps induct me into the Texas Country Music Hall of Fame

My golfing pals, Front row (L to R) Johnny McCullah, Guido, Larry Mac, Tom Buster. Back row (L to R) Bill White, Warren Beroughenmoughorboorug, Fun Cart Jeff, and my ol' buddy Dave Cox. I told you guys I would make you famous!

My friend Rick Sutcliffe, The Red Baron

Hook 'em Horns!

Photo courtest of J.M. Furco

On Stage

Photo courtest of J.M. Furco

A successful hunting trip with my pals Snuffy Garrett and Larry Buxton

With my dear Aunt Mary

On the Country's Family Reunion Cruise with TG Sheppard, Kelly Lang, Jeannie Seely, Rhonda Vincent, Moe Bandy and Mark Wills

Cruising with Mark Wills and Bill Anderson

One of my favorite photos of my son Connor

At a school event
with Connor

A typical day with Connor. Seeing who could eat the most hard boiled eggs

Yeah I love being on stage with my daughter Cherish

On the Opry with Cherish just after she announced she was pregnant

**Office of the Mayor
for the City of La Marque**

PROCLAMATION

WHEREAS, born "Johnny Lee" Ham, in Texas City, Texas on July 3, 1946, and grew up in Alta Loma, Texas; and

WHEREAS, after high school, his first band, "The Roadrunners", performed in is area, before he enlisted in the United States Navy, where he proudly served his country in a tour of duty in southeast Asia;

WHEREAS, in 1968, he began his 10 year working relationship with Mickey Gilley at the world famous nightclub "Gilley's" in Pasadena, Texas; and in 1979 he was asked to perform "Looking for Love" in the film "Urban Cowboy", which later became his first Gold Record; and

WHEREAS, he has rich roots in this area and is also a long-time friend of the Mayor Hocking of La Marque (fifty years); and

WHEREAS; he has been a featured performer of the Annual La Marque Bayou Fest since the beginning; and

SO BE IT RESOLVED, we consider him "One in a Million" in this community; as he continues to perform, to this day, in Branson Missouri and many other cities throughout the State of Texas; and

NOW, THEREFORE, we the Mayor and City Council by virtue of our authority vested by the City of La Marque, Texas do hereby proclaim July 3rd of each calendar year:

"JOHNNY LEE" DAY

In testimony whereof, witness my hand and the Seal of the City of La Marque, this the 15th day of October 2016.

Bobby Hocking
Bobby Hocking, Mayor

Each July 3rd is Johnny Lee Day in La Marque, Texas

Always having fun on stage

My Band Members

Tony Walter

Mike Crosno

Sean Alders

Rickey Caron

Johnnie Helms

Scot England meets Johnny Lee 1987. Almost 30 years later, Scot would help me write this book.

With Jaclyn (Es Day By God Lauder) Duncan

Standin' on the corner in Winslow, Arizona

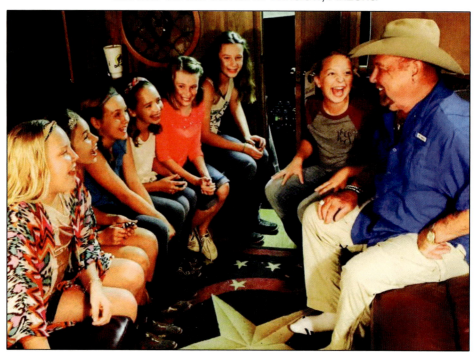

Surprised on my bus by a group of school girls in Crawford, Texas.
I love their faces!

My grandson Wyatt smiles as I sing to him for the first time

Wyatt holds his grandpa's hand

Who would have thought that Johnny Lee and Charlene Tilton would be proud grandparents!

It was love at first sight

My grandson makes his Opry debut. Nov. 25, 2016

My grandson has inherited his grandpa's hairline!

CHAPTER TWENTY TWO

Adults Only!

Lots of people say they are going to tell EVERYTHING in their autobiography, but they never do! And when their book comes out, you can tell that it's a glossed-over, cleaned up, make-them-sound-like-an-angel version of their life.

They only tell you half of the truth! But my mama always told me that a half-truth was the same as a complete lie. So I wanted to be honest in my book. I wanted to tell the truth. I know I am not perfect… very far from it. So why try to fool people?

The truth is, the life of a country star is not always pretty. And some of the things those of us who were high-rolling in the 70s and 80s saw and did… they would make most of today's hot stars run crying to their mommies!

This chapter is for Adults Only! That means it is not for kids! It is also not for those who are offended by strong language and some sexual content.

The last thing I want is for any of my fans to take offense or get upset over something I say. So I have made it easy, and put all of the adult content in this one chapter. If you do not want to read the next few stories, just thumb on by and go to the next chapter.

I am the most politically incorrect human being you will ever meet.

But I tell people that I am not politically incorrect... I am delightfully inappropriate.

I say what's on my mind.

But I do not want one of my longtime female fans, ones who are now great grandmas, coming up to me saying, "Johnny, I loved your book until that Adults Only chapter. I can't believe you put all of that horrible stuff in there! It completely ruined your book. I will never listen to your songs again."

So PLEASE, if you think there is even the slightest chance you will be offended, just skip over the next seven or eight pages.

So here's the deal.

I have given you fair warning.

If you continue reading the rest of this chapter, you will find out exactly how it was to be one of the hottest country music stars in the world.

Don't blame me. I warned ya.

My first idea for a book title was "Y'all Ain't Gonna Believe This Shit!"

But they said it wouldn't work. I thought it would be an eye-catcher.

Speaking of eye-catcher...

Mickey Gilley didn't like us playing poker on the bus. His main reason was that every night, whoever lost all their money would come to Gilley and ask for a loan.

One night, one of my guitar players, Little Henry, was the one who lost all of his money. He didn't want to go to Mickey, so he ended up betting the only thing that he had left... his glass eye!

We were all pretty drunk, so we thought, "if a guy wants to bet his glass eye, so be it". Another band member, Mike Shillaci, took him up on the bet. And Mike won.

A few minutes later, we were all grossed out, as one-eyed Henry sat staring at us.

Right then, Mike came out from the back of the bus. He turned around, bent over, and pulled his pants down. He had stuck that glass eye in his ass! He said, "Here's lookin' at you, Henry!"

Henry freaked out. He knew he was gonna have to put his eye back in for the show!

John Daly had a celebrity golf tournament, and after we'd spent the day on the golf course, he hosted a big banquet dinner.

I was seated at the head table. It was a huge table, with about 25 people sitting around it. It looked like the Last Supper.

I was sitting next to some girl I met, and John Daly was sitting next to me on the other side.

During dinner, my date whispered in my ear, "Johnny, I would do anything for you."

For some reason I replied, "You would? Would you get down on your knees under the table right now?"

She looked at me and said, "Oh, I just dropped my fork." And she slipped under the table. I put my cloth napkin over my lap.

Right then, a fiddle player came over to the table and stood by us. He was followed by a guitar player, and they both played right over us. They were trying to impress John Daly and me.

I leaned over to John and whispered, "If you think they are impressive, look at this." And I lifted my table napkin. My date had her face in my lap, doing her thing.

John's eyes about popped out of his head and I said, "Well, this is the Head table isn't it?!"

I was on hole 17 at Pointe Royale in Branson. It's a par 3. I hit a shot that landed on the green. But it rolled off the green, went down the hill, across the golf cart path and the ball landed in the lake.

I yelled, "You cocksucker!" That hole is in a little valley. And when you say something it echoes all through the valley. So when I yelled that, there was this sweet little lady who was working in her garden next to the course. She turned around and looked at me. I said, "Sorry about the cocksucker ma'am."

I was once playing golf with a female Japanese golf star, and she couldn't speak any English. My friend, Walt Garrison, was also in the tournament, and I was talking to him before the event.

Walt told me that the only Japanese he knew would be something I could say to her if she happened to hit a bad shot. He gave me the saying. He said that it meant, "That's OK pro. That's OK."

I memorized it, and about halfway through our match, she hit a poor shot. So I stepped right up and loudly said the phrase that Walt had given me. That girl shot me a look and then took off walking. Her caddie looked like he wanted to kill me. She didn't even get close to me for the rest of the match.

That night, I told Walt that she had gotten mad. He was drinking a Coke at the time, and it came out of his nose when he yelled, "You didn't really say that to her?!" He said, "You told her, 'Your pussy smells like rice'!"

I had a blind bass player. His name was Bill. He was a great player, and a great singer, but he was blind as a bat.

Right before we went on, Bill told me that he had to go to the bathroom. I knew we were about a minute away from the show starting, so I led him backstage to a nearby closet. I walked him into the closet and shut the door. I stood outside and I could hear him feeling around in there. And then he yelled, "Hey! This shit ain't funny! I'm going to piss all over everything!"

I started laughing, and finally opened the door and took him to the closest bathroom.

To help pass the time on the road, we would play a game called "Would ya?"

When we'd pass by a woman, we'd ask each other, "Would ya?" That meant, "Would you do her or not?"

One time, we were walking behind a woman with long black hair. She had a nice figure, and I poked my band member Tommy and said, "Would ya?"

Tommy answered, "Most definitely!"

Just then, the 'woman' turned around. And it was a Chinese boy!

Every now and then, a reporter will ask me, "What is the weirdest thing you have ever been asked to autograph?" I have never told them the truth, but I will now.

A guy asked me to sign his dick. I said, "I don't know if I can do that, but I will initial it." I didn't.

I've signed babies. I felt weird, signing a baby with a damn Sharpie.

I signed a girl's shoulder once, and she had my signature tattooed on her.

And I've signed all kinds of titties. I'm a titty fan. I love titties.

This girl came up to me in the autograph line at a show in Texas and she had two big bottles of Crown Royal, one in each hand. She said, "Johnny, would you sign my jugs?"

I said, "I sure will, if you'll put those Crown Royal bottles down!"

I was married to Charlene Tilton at the time.

Me and my pal Bobby were in England, and we were staying in a big hotel.

Bobby came over to me at dinner, and in his low, slow voice, he said "Hey Johnny... How about you and me go downtown... and get us some pussy?"

I shook my head and said, "Bobby, I can't do it. I've got the best pussy in the world waiting for me at home."

Bobby sat there for a couple seconds, and then he said, "Well Johnny... let's go to your house."

Sherwood Cryer would never turn the air conditioning on at Gilley's. He always said, "If people are sweating their balls off, they will buy more beer."

Sherwood once bet a drunk guy $500 that he couldn't sit on a block of ice and jack off. It can't be done.

I once wrote what I thought was the perfect country love song. It was called "If your heart was as big as your ass, you'd take me back".

I wrote the song and made a single out of it! You can buy a copy on my website at johnnyleemusic.com

Mickey and I were so hot that the Schlitz Brewing beer company in Milwaukee asked us to do some commercials for them. They had agreed to pay us $50,000 to appear in the ads, and they said that we could cut the commercials in Nashville.

The company officials were very excited about me and Mickey being a part of the Schlitz family. We were touring in Florida, and they asked us to come tour the Schlitz plant in Jacksonville.

We had a big group, and their press people were taking pictures of us as we walked through the plant. The head of the plant was telling us what all the different machines did. The guy said, "This is the dryer for the bottles."

I yelled, "They don't have a dik-fer?!"

Over the roar of the bottling machines, the manager loudly asked me, "What's a dik-fer?"

I yelled back, "Fer fuckin'!"

That was it. The tour was over. The commercials came to an end, and so did our $50,000. Just from that one comment.

I had Captain Sid playing bass for me. I went up to him and asked if he had anything to give me some energy. I was dog tired. He said, "Yeah, I've got something."

He slipped his hand around mine so that no one would see him give me anything, and he whispered, "Wash this down with some whiskey."

I started to feel it with my fingers, without looking down at my hand. I thought that it felt a little spongy. Just as I was about to put it in my mouth, I opened my hand and saw that it was a wart! Sidney had given me a wart he had just taken off of his hand. I said, "Sidney, if I would have eaten that thing, I would have beaten the shit out of you. I will get you back."

A long time later, Jerry Lee Lewis came to Gilley's. The Killer was known for having good drugs, and backstage, he gave me a pill that looked like a big green jelly bean. It was a Placidyl. It was a horse tranquilizer. I wasn't about to take that thing, but I saved it.

One night, Captain Sid came up to me and said, "Boss, I am tired."

I said, "This will do the trick," as I gave him that pill that Jerry Lee had given me.

He had a hard time swallowing it, but he got it down. And just before he walked on stage to play with Mickey Gilley, that stuff hit him.

He was playing bass, but he just stood there. He couldn't move.

Mickey thought he was playing around, and started to give him some angry looks. Finally, Mickey stopped and said, "Sidney, what is wrong with you?!"

Sid very slowly said, "I can't move my fingers. I know what to do, but I can't get my fingers there." He looked at me and asked, "How long will this last?"

I said, "Two days bitch! Remember that wart?"

Another funny story about Sid: one night, Sid was in bed with a woman. In the middle of the night, he got out of bed to go to the bathroom, so I thought that I would play a trick on Sid and his girl. As she slept, I quietly slid into Sid's spot in the bed. I didn't have a shirt on, and if you've ever seen me with no shirt, I am pretty hairy. It's like I still have a sweater on. In the dark room, Sid's girl started feeling my chest. She felt all that hair and she started screaming, "Who the hell is this?!"

When I was performing in England, I took three armadillos from Texas with me. I was going to give them to a zoo in England. And as I was getting ready to present the armadillos to the head of the zoo, one of them shit right in my pants pocket.

I named the three armadillos Eeny, Meeny and Miny. There was no Mo!

I was once visiting with one of my best friends, Snuffy Garrett.

I said, "Snuffy, back when I was famous, back in the Gilley's days, back when I was purty... I was getting laid more than the Los Angeles Lakers, Secretariat and Elvis Presley all put together."

Snuffy looked at me and said, "More than all of them put together? What the hell happened? Why ain't we getting laid now?"

Me and Mickey Gilley were doing a show in Oklahoma. At the end of the show, I was reaching down to shake people's hands. There was one woman reaching up for me but she was too far back and I couldn't reach her. I was afraid I might fall off the stage if I leaned out any further.

Later in my autograph line, she came up and said, "I was the one who was trying to shake your hand. But you were afraid I was going to jerk you off."

I asked, "What?" She said, "You were afraid I was going to jerk you off."

I said, "No ma'am. This is the autograph line. That line is over there!"

All of the above stories are true. But the following are a few "Johnny Jokes".

My friend Hollywood Clayton called me, and said, "Johnny, I just had the craziest night of my life! I made love to a set of twins." He said the only way he could tell them apart was that one had a mustache… her brother!

I was dating a fat woman. The back of her neck had so many rolls that it looked like a pack of wieners.

I wrote a song about a homeless girl I used to date. The best thing about dating a homeless girl is... at the end of the date, you can drop her anywhere.

A little boy was in the backyard with his grandpa. The boy found an earthworm, and was trying to put it back in its hole.

His grandpa says, "I bet you five dollars that you can't get that worm back in there. It's too limp and wiggly". The little boy thought about it a minute, and then ran inside and got a big can of his grandma's Aqua Net hairspray. He sprayed that worm until it was straight and stiff as a board. Then he put it right into the hole.

Grandpa hands the boy a five dollar bill, grabs the hairspray, and runs into the house. A half-hour later, he comes back and gives the boy another five dollars.

The boy says "Grandpa, you already gave me the money."

His Grandpa smiled and said, "That's from your grandma."

I love T.G. Sheppard and his wife Kelly Lang. T.G. told me they were going to Greece. I said, "That's great."

T.G. said, "Yeah, we ran out of K-Y jelly." (You have to say that joke out loud to get it.)

One Christmas, three Arkansas rednecks were hit by a train and killed.

Saint Peter met them at the Pearly Gates. He told them, "Since it is almost Christmas, and the big guy is in a good mood, if you have anything on you that symbolizes the spirit of Christmas, I will let you in."
The first redneck pulled out the keys to his pickup truck. He said, "These symbolize the bells of Christmas."

Saint Peter said, "That's good. Come on in."

The second guy reached in his pocket and found his zippo lighter. He flicked the flame up and said, "This symbolizes the lights of Christmas."

Saint Peter told him to go on in.

The third redneck thought and thought, and finally he pulled out a pair of ladies' panties.

Saint Peter asked, "What is this?"

The guy said, "They're Carol's."

My grandpa Wilson was my hero. His nickname was Chick. When Grandpa was 98 years old, he had a 24 year old girlfriend, whose name was Gloria. Grandpa told Gloria that he wanted to marry her, and she told him, "If you can father my children, I will marry you."

The next day, he went to the doctor, and told him that he needed to be able to father a child. The doctor told him he needed to give a specimen.

They gave him a jar, and sent him to a room at the end of the hall.

A half-hour went by. The nurse looked at the clock. 45 minutes went by. Finally, an hour passed. The nurse asked the doctor, "Do you think he is OK?"

The doctor said, "He is 98. Give him a few more minutes."

After an hour and a half, the doctor knocked on the door.

Grandpa was out of breath, as he opened the door. He was breathing hard. He said, "Doc, I tried for 20 minutes with my left hand. I wore my hand out. Then I switched to my right hand for 20 minutes. My hand was almost numb." He said, "Doc, I ran hot water over it. I even banged it on the top of the counter and… I just can not get the lid off of this jar!"

CHAPTER TWENTY THREE

Family Time

Imagine yourself as a "Country Star". You are on stage, or walking down the street. You are going along, just being yourself, when you hear some redneck jackass say, "He thinks he's hot shit."

Let me set the record straight right here… that redneck jackass could not be more wrong! I can be so insecure. And many other artists are, as well. I have a true need to be loved by everyone. I don't want anybody to not like me. I can be in a room of 5,000 fans who all love me, but if one asshole comes up and says something negative to me, I will focus on that. I will forget all about the 5,000 people who love me, and only remember that one jerk who doesn't. I'm sure there is a mental term for that, but I know it is a problem for me, and I am trying to get over that.

The one person who I have tried to please more than anyone else in my life is my mother. Throughout my life and career, I have loved sharing my success and good times with her. When I made it big, I wanted to reward my mom in every way that I could. She had worked so hard all of her life.

When I played Reno, I flew her and her husband out there. And when Charlene and I were married in Lake Tahoe, of course my mom was there.

She stayed a lot with us in California, and helped take care of Cherish when she was a baby.

For Mother's Day one year, I took her to Hawaii. I also took her on her first cruise. We went to the Caribbean, and to Mexico.

One year, I surprised my mom with a special gift. She looked confused, as she opened a purple raincoat and rubber boots. I told her to look inside the coat pocket, and she pulled out plane tickets to Alaska.

When mother was a little girl living in Oklahoma during the

Depression years, her Dad could not find a job anywhere, so he ended up going all the way to Alaska, where he got a job building the Alkan highway. Mom always wanted to go to Alaska so that she could see what her Daddy saw there.

My son JL also went with us. I had always wanted to take my son on a big fishing trip. We went fishing in Valdez, and caught the biggest salmon. My son caught one with his bare hands, and we caught so many fish, there was no way we could bring them all back home with us. We had to have them shipped back.

We stayed at the Captain Cook Hotel, where I ate musk ox for the first time.

We walked through glaciers. It was amazing.

We all had such a wonderful time, and I am so thankful for that wonderful memory with my son and my mother. It was a time that I will always treasure.

Even after all my success, my mom was still working hard. She worked for Southwest Research, in the automotive department, where she was a test car driver. She'd drive a car for 8 hours a day in order to test the gas mileage, the brakes, and everything else. Sometimes, she'd follow a route through residential areas and downtown, and other days, she would just drive in a circle in a parking lot.

Mom worked her way up in the company, but as she advanced, she was embarrassed because she didn't even have a high school education. She was working with all of these engineers who had impressive college degrees, and she hadn't even gotten through high school. So she went back and got her GED. My mother has always been an inspiration to me.

On my mom's 80th birthday, I couldn't be with her, so I had all of my friends call her. I went through my entire rolodex, and had almost 100 people call her! She was on the phone the entire day! She got calls from Crystal Gayle, Jim Ed Brown, John Daly, Lane Brody, Ed Bruce, Ace Cannon, Jack Greene, Larry Gatlin, Roy Clark, Mickey Gilley, Moe Bandy, Barbara Fairchild, TG Sheppard, and even the host of 'Jeopardy', Alex Trebeck!

I love all of my brothers and sisters. Even though we all had different fathers, we really bonded as true siblings. My youngest brother, Jimmy, lives in Florida, and I am real close with him. He is a very kindhearted guy. I had a D-76 Martin guitar, and I gave it to Jimmy. I wrote him a note with the guitar, and he broke down crying when he read it. He made me cry too, because he was so emotional about it.

My sister Claudia lives in Texas. She and I are close and I love her very much. Janet and Jan are twins. Of course I have to love them an equal amount!

If you have seen me in concert over the last 20 years, chances are you have also seen my brother Lynn or my sister Jan.

Lynn sold T-shirts, pictures and other merchandise at my shows for many years. He actually made the shirts as he sold them. He printed them right on the bus as we traveled!

I loved having Lynn on the road with me, and I knew I could always trust him. He was never envious of my success. He did his thing, and I did mine. And we have grown closer together as the years have gone on.

Lynn is quite a fisherman. And in recent years, he has been a professional fishing guide. But for some reason, he won't let me borrow his fishing gear. He did once, and when I'd brought it back, the fishing lines were all wadded in knots, and a pole or two was broken. I told him, "These are crappy rods and reels."

Lynn said, "No, the rods are fine. It's the person who doesn't know how to use them." The next day, I wanted to borrow his gear again, and he said, "You go rent your own."

In 2014, Lynn wanted to get off the road, so my sister Jan took over selling my merchandise. Back when I was starting out, when we were getting ready to play a dance, I'd go buy a 45 record and have her write down all the words for me. And that's something that continues today. If I need the words to a song, she'll type them up for me. She'll put the words on a sheet of paper at the front of the stage. But these days, she has to make the print so big so that I can see it! Sometimes, one song might be on 5 or 6 feet of paper all across the front of the stage!

Jan is nine years younger than me. We were hardly ever together when we were younger, but now we are together all the time. She lives with me in Branson, and she also oversees all of my websites, social media, and mail. She also takes care of all of my travel scheduling. She basically tells me where to go! I know I can trust her with all of my business affairs.

Jan also sings backup on the song 'Cherokee Fiddle' during my concerts. She'll be sitting behind the merch table, but as soon as she hears the first notes of 'Cherokee Fiddle' start to play, she turns into a Dallas Cowboy linebacker. She drops everything she's doing, and runs to the stage. Don't ever get in her way!

So what's it been like to be with your big brother almost 24 hours a day for the past few years? I'll let Jan tell it….

"I was in the third grade when Johnny went into the Navy. It was so hard on all of us kids to watch him go away, especially with the war going on.

When my twin sister Janet and I were 17 years old, we went to see Johnny at Gilley's. We were too young to drink, but men kept coming over, offering us drinks and asking us to dance. Johnny was watching from the stage, and he finally came over and asked the men to leave us alone.

I never doubted that Johnny would make it in music. But I was pleasantly surprised when he became such a huge star! Me and my husband were in the Air Force, and stationed in Italy, when 'Urban Cowboy' came out. So we missed the first couple of years of Johnny's huge success. When we got back from Italy, he was already married to a Hollywood star, Charlene Tilton, and their daughter was about to be born.

I never get tired of hearing him sing his songs. I love going to all of his shows. I like traveling with him. I love every minute of it. I love watching the fans.

When I started working on the road with Johnny, I found out that one of my jobs was trying to keep up all of his women 'friends'. He would have different 'friends', who all thought they were his number one. He would have different ones at each venue, in each town and in each state!

One night, there were two different ladies who came to the concert. They both thought they were Johnny's one and only girl. He didn't want to hurt either one of them, so while one waited, he visited with one on the bus. When they were through, as she left, the other one walked on. Johnny looked at me and rolled his eyes. I walked away as I heard him say, 'Hello Darlin…'

When I first moved in with him, he still had his landline phone. Cell phones hadn't started yet. And different women would call. Some would call so much that he finally said, 'When you answer the phone, you need to pretend that we are married. Tell them you are my wife and that they shouldn't call here again.'

But that was years ago, and he has slowed down a lot since he turned 70.

He loves his fans so much. He will sit there for an hour and a half signing autographs and taking pictures. He never gets tired of talking to his fans. He will not leave until the last person is gone.

People will ask me, 'Will he sign autographs?'

I say, 'Yes, he always does.'

Then they ask, 'What won't he sign?'

I tell them, 'When I see him turn something down, I'll let you know.'

I've seen him sign boobs and butts, backs and fronts. He has signed a lot of body parts.

I probably know Johnny better than anyone, just because we are always together. And I've learned a lot about him, as a person, as a man, and as a father. Yes, he is a little gruff sometimes. But he is so tenderhearted. He has such a huge heart. And he is an incredibly kind, generous, giving soul.

– Jan Cerny

Jan mentioned me signing autographs. Every now and then, someone will have me sign their arm or something, and then they'll go have the autograph turned into a tattoo. You know someone is a true fan when they do something like that.

I have quite a few tattoos, and when I was growing up, I never thought that I'd get any.

I have a Road Runner on my right arm. I got that the first night I was on liberty in the Navy. I got that for my group Johnny Lee and the Roadrunners.

On my left arm, I have a big tattoo that I got when I went to Vietnam. It was supposed to be a little devil breathing fire, holding a pitchfork, and it said 'Black Gangs Hell'. That was our division. The guy who gave me the tattoo was drunker than I was. You couldn't read it, and it looked like a pig with a fish stuck in its mouth. I got tired of people asking what it was, so I had a guy in Las Vegas cover it up. He covered it up with a big 'Cherish' and 'JL 2'.

The one on my lower left arm is my son. I wish I had waited, because it really doesn't look like him. I got it in Roswell, New Mexico. It's my son and his dog Zoey.

I have the word 'HOPE' on my knuckles, with one letter on each finger. I did that in honor of my son. My son also loved penguins, so I had a penguin tattooed onto my lower right arm. If I ever get married again, I'll get a mate for that penguin and put them next to each other.

And I have my own camel toe! I have a camel tattoo on my big toe. Let me tell you something… don't ever get a tattoo on your toe! It hurts like hell. The tattoo guy made me promise I wouldn't kick him in the head. It was painful.

Cherish and I have matching tattoos. When she was a little girl, she wore those fake tattoos. He mom told her she couldn't get a real one until she turned 18. Well, Cherish happened to be with me on her 18th birthday. To celebrate we found this hole in the wall tattoo place and told the guy we wanted tattoos. He turned us down because we had been drinking. So we asked what he drank. He said tequila, so we bought him some and boom! We got our damn tattoos!

We chose a dolphin jumping through a wave, but it's hard to tell what they are.

They were supposed to be on our ankles, but the guy missed by about six inches, and they are up our lower legs. They're nearly in the middle of our damn leg! But we both agreed that we wouldn't get them covered up.

You shouldn't be drunk when you go and get a tattoo, but your tattoo artist should not be drunk either.

CHAPTER TWENTY FOUR

Hit Songs

I have been blessed to have a lot of hit songs. Most of those came over an almost 10 year period from 1977 to 1986. Of course, I am still recording, and even though my new songs might never make the top ten on the charts, I think the songs that I did on my last album are just as good, if not better, than many of the hits I had back in the 80s.

As I look back at my career, here are some of my thoughts about my biggest hits.

1977   Country Party - I re-wrote Ricky Nelson's big hit 'Garden Party'. I had the chance to sing it for Ricky, and he gave his blessing to me. That meant the world to me. It made it to #15 on the charts. It didn't set the world on fire, but it was a good start for me.

1980   Lookin' for Love -I knew it was a hit. And of course, it was at number one for a few weeks, but I couldn't have dreamed that it would have the impact on my life that it did. Not many people know this, but I actually did a Spanish version of the song as well. I had never spoken Spanish, but I wrote it out phonetically and did it.

1980   One in a Million -It went to number one, and is still one of my signature songs. Whenever I start singing it, people always remember it within the first couple notes. I am very thankful for that.

1981   Pickin' Up Strangers - It was used in a movie called 'Coast to Coast'. The movie starred Robert Blake and Dyan Cannon. T.G. Sheppard sang the theme song of the movie, but 'Pickin' Up Strangers' was the song that became a hit. For some reason, a lot of kids like that song. My most memorable performance of 'Pickin' Up

Strangers' was at a 4th of July party. I was playing the song on my guitar, and just when I started singing, a June bug flew into my ear. There is nothing more painful! That bug started going deep in my ear, and every time it moved, I screamed. I thought it was going to go into my brain or try to come out my eye! They finally had to take me to the hospital to get it out.

1981   Prisoner of Hope - A Jim Ed Norman song. It went to number 3 on the charts. I wasn't in love with anyone at this time, but I would always pretend that I was singing it to someone I loved.

1981   Be There For Me Baby - Another Jim Ed Norman song. My mother loved that song. I thought it was a hit as soon as I heard it. And it made it into the top ten.

1982   When You Fall In Love - That song should have went a lot higher than it did. It only went to #14. But it was a good song.

1982   Cherokee Fiddle - Another top ten song. I wanted to release this for a long time before they finally did. Sneaky Pete, who played with The Flying Burrito Brothers, played steel guitar on the track. John Boylan produced the song, but Jim Ed Norman had Sneaky Pete taken off. He said it was too rock and roll. Michael Martin Murphey wrote the song. Michael also sang harmony on it. Charlie Daniels played fiddle, and Rosemary Butler, who sang with Jackson Brown, sang the girl's part.

1982   Sounds Like Love - I'm still not crazy about that song. I hate singing it during my shows. It was just a bubble gum song to me. I was pre-warned to watch what you record, because if it becomes a hit, you'll have to sing it for the rest of your life. And this was a big hit, after it went all the way to number 6. But the song really doesn't do it for me.

1983   Hey Bartender - Kenny Fulton sang it at Gilley's, and I liked it. He told me he had heard it on the Blues Brothers album, but I found out that Floyd Dixon had written it way back during the prohibition. My record company didn't want to release it, because it had saxophone on it. I told them, "This is my career. If I want to hang myself, I'll be the one to kick the horse." After it hit the top of the charts, Floyd Dixon told me, "I like your version… and I like the checks that it's bringing."

1983   My Baby Don't Slow Dance - It was a little boogie woogie. I wish I could re-record that song. I would do it a lot better. At the time, we were so busy and so rushed, we were trying to record in-between our concerts. But I really like that song.

1983   The Yellow Rose - A number one duet for Lane Brody and I. It was the theme song for the TV show 'The Yellow Rose', which starred Cybil Shepherd and Sam Elliot. 'The Yellow Rose' was not supposed to be a single. I had a song called 'Say When', and that was the song that was supposed to be the 'A' side. But on the flip side of the 45, we put 'The Yellow Rose'.

And for some reason, all the radio stations started playing it. And they played it all the way to number one. I couldn't believe it. It's weird to dance to, but people still love it.

1984   One More Shot - I just dug this song. But things were starting to taper off with radio. It only got to number 42. New artists like Dwight Yoakam were taking over the radio spots. When your songs start dropping off the charts, it is always one of two things: it's either the fans are tired of you, or your record company is tired of you. And it is usually the second thing. That's the way the record business is.

Of course, Dwight Yoakam, the guy who took my place on the charts, his time came and went. His hits stopped, and new people came to take his place. But the talent is still there, and the fans of Dwight and all of my fans are still there, even if we never have another hit.

1984   You Could've Heard a Heart Break - I had one more number one song in me! I have a lot of fun with this song. I always ask the crowd if anyone has been caught cheating. You'd be surprised how many hands go up!

1985   Rollin' Lonely - This rolled all the way to the top ten on the charts. It is a song that I relate to, because I was also on the road all the time. It can get mighty lonely going down that interstate, especially late at night.

1985   Save The Last Chance - I love this song. My band that I tour with now has probably never heard it. I need to put it back in my show.

1985   They Never Had To Get Over You - This is a great, great song. Mike McGuire, the drummer from Shenandoah, was a co-writer on that song.

1986   I Could Get Used To This - This was a beautiful ballad. It was really a different style than what I usually did, but it turned out very nice. It was a second duet with Lane Brody, and we had thought that if we had a number one song in 1983, we might capture the magic once again. We did our part, and the song deserved to be a big hit, but the music business had changed over the last three years. My record company didn't support or promote the song, and it only managed to make it to #50 on the charts.

I have also recorded a lot of songs that people wouldn't have thought that I would sing. I did a number of songs on my albums, and they were never released as singles, but they turned out to be big hits for other people.

As I mentioned earlier, I did 'Do You Love As Good As You Look' before The Bellamy Brothers released it. I also had 'I Can Tell By The Way You Dance', which was a number one for Vern Gosdin. I also recorded 'Come As You Were', which turned out to be a great song for T. Graham Brown.

And can you believe that I recorded two Elton John songs? I did 'Your Song' and 'I Guess That's Why They Call It The Blues'. I'm not a big Elton John fan, but I love his music. And I think I did those songs well.

The Huey Lewis song 'Workin' For a Living' was the title cut from one of my albums. I also recorded the Jim Croce classic 'I'll Have To Say I Love You In A Song'. I did that one just because I wanted to sing it. It's one of my favorite songs.

CHAPTER TWENTY FIVE

The Future

I turned 70 years old on July 3, 2016. 70 years old!

It sounds different. It doesn't feel any different. But it sounds weird when I say it. It might scare some of my younger lady friends when they find out I'm 70.

A few people have asked, "Are you ever going to retire?" and I tell them, "I can either keep singing, or get a job as a greeter at Walmart. And if they keep raising the minimum wage, that's not out of the question!"

If you would have told me 40 years ago that I would live to be 70, I probably wouldn't have believed you. So, I guess I have really beaten the odds. Most of my hard-partying days are over. A little bit of partying goes a long way these days.

Speaking of parties, I played in Granbury, Texas the night before my 70th birthday. They brought me out a cake, and my agent gave me a half gallon of Jack Daniels whiskey. They sat it on the stage, but I waited until the show was almost over before I had a couple drinks.

We were on the road on the bus at midnight as I turned 70. I got home at about 10:00 in the morning, had a quiet day, and then spent the evening watching fireworks from my balcony overlooking Table Rock Lake. I also spent that night talking to friends on the phone. I got so many calls and messages. I finally had to just turn my phone off, or else I would have never gotten any sleep. I am so blessed to have so many people who love me. To have that many people want to wish you a happy birthday, that makes me feel good. I thought that was a pretty good way to celebrate my 70th birthday.

But I had no idea that my birthday celebration had only just begun!

A few days later, one of my buddies, Tom Buster came by. Tom asked me to go uptown to see a couple of friends. We went to a little bar, and had a couple drinks. I had no clue what was going on at my house while I was gone.

My sister Jan and my daughter Cherish had planned a huge surprise party. They had all of the guests park down the street, and when I got home, there was no sign of anyone. When I walked in, everyone started yelling "Surprise!"

I actually cried. It was a very emotional time to see all my friends there. More than 100 people were there. They came in from Las Vegas, Wisconsin, Oklahoma, Texas, Arkansas, and even Arizona. It was great.

It was the first birthday party I've had since I was a kid. I was usually working and couldn't get off for my birthday, and since it is always around the 4th of July weekend, everyone is usually busy doing other things.

Just before my birthday, I bought myself a new recliner. It's like that George Jones song: "I don't need no rockin' chair." But I did need a nice recliner. When I come home, I like to do some mechanical work on my recliner… I put a rear end in that thing.

I live in Branson, Missouri, but I don't work in Branson very much. Most of the entertainers who live there also have theaters there, but I just enjoy living there. Everybody knows me there. When I go out anywhere in town, the people know me, and I like that.

When he was really hot in Branson, Mickey Gilley offered me a job at his theater. I can't say that I regret not doing it, but I think maybe I should have. But at the time, I was making more money in one night on the road than I could have made in a week in Branson.

But in late 2016, I agreed to play in Branson with Mickey three days a week for two months. We filled in for Mel Tillis on dates that he had booked before he had gotten sick.

Those shows with Mickey helped us close out 2016 on a very high note. Crowds packed the theater almost every show we did. The dates were so successful that we agreed to come back and do a bunch more shows together in 2017. Those will be at the Mickey Gilley Theatre, so please come see us!

Timeshares are big in Branson. Have you ever sat through a timeshare meeting? I have… many of them! Can you believe I actually sold timeshares for one year!

I wasn't working the road much at the time, and a man who was the head of a timeshare company told me, "You would be a natural. People will buy these from you just because you are Johnny Lee!"

I went through the sessions, to learn how to sell. I bought one for myself. I got it at a discount, and then I couldn't wait to get rid of the son of a bitch.

I made sales to the first seven people that I met with. I said, "Damn, this is easy!"

But believe it or not, I got tired of talking all day long. I know that's hard to believe, but my voice would get tired, and I got tired of trying to convince people to buy something that they didn't really need. It wasn't for me. It just wasn't my bag. And some of the people who would come in had been fans of mine, and they would say, "What the hell are you doing selling timeshares?"

I told them, "I'm an owner. I believe in them." I was successful at it at first, but it got old quick.

I am a Texan. I was born in Texas. I am a Texan at heart. But Branson is my home.

For a long time, I didn't really like Branson. But I came to find out that there are a lot of really good people here. I have some life-long friends here. I have people here who would do anything for me.

I grew to love it in Branson. I love the lakes. I have a beautiful home that overlooks the lake. I love the seasons.

My son went to school in Branson, and I still see a lot of his friends. Branson is my son's final resting place. And it will be my final resting place, too.

But I am a long way from resting.

I did over 100 concerts in 2016. I had so many shows that I had to buy a new tour bus! I'll play a garage door opening if someone pays me. If I'm offered a job and I don't take it, I know that someone else will.

People still want to hire me. People still come to see me. And I would be a fool to turn anyone down. I love doing shows. And I love having a week or so off every now and then, but at the end of the week, I'm ready to get out and go.

I am so busy that I cannot keep up with all the stuff we are doing. I just have to refer anyone's interview or concert requests to my agent. This past year, I also found time to record and release a new CD, 'You Ain't Never Been To Texas'.

It was my first CD in ten years. I had so many hits before, there was no need to do any new music. I knew that people came out to hear my old songs, so I had taken a long break from recording. But I finally felt that it was time to do something new. I wanted to do something that was real, solid country.

Some people are kind of dumb when they ask you, "Is your new CD any good?"

I want to say, "No! I thought I would do a bunch of crap this time!"

I financed my CD myself. I had never done anything like this on my own. Buddy Wyatt helped me produce the album, and it turned out to be one of the best things that I have ever recorded.

People always ask me, "Do you have any goals that you have not reached yet?"

Sure I do. I still want to write a classic song. And I want to write a great book. You can be the judge of that one. If this wasn't great enough, I can start working on my next 70 years.

I also have one very big goal.

I have always dreamed of being a member of the Grand Ole Opry. Since I live in Branson, a long way from Nashville, I haven't been able to play the Opry very much, but every time I'm on the show, they always ask me to come back and do it more. And I would love to be a member of that family.

That's my dream. Maybe if I start playing the Opry more often, that will remind them that I'm still out there entertaining the crowds. I love doing the Opry. It's an honor. That's the only place where I ever get nervous before I walk out on stage.

It kills me to not be a member of the Opry. I know they try to get the new, young artists. They think they will draw in a crowd. And they do, but Johnny Lee can still draw a crowd. And Johnny Lee has more hits than most of the new guys will ever have!

By the way, on November 25, 2016, my grandson made his debut on the Opry stage. Wyatt was one month old when my daughter carried him out to meet me at the center of the Ryman Auditorium stage. It was one of the true highlights of my life. Wyatt slept through it.

Will I ever get married again? I won't say that I won't. But I haven't got any plans to remarry anytime soon. I hope to meet a true companion one day. I'd love to find someone to spend the rest of my life with. And if I ever meet somebody, hopefully I'll know that she is the right one.

But until that day comes… as the title of this book says, yes, I am still Lookin' for Love. Aren't we all?

CHAPTER TWENTY SIX

Parting Song

Like most people, I became a fan of Johnny Lee when I first heard 'Lookin' for Love'. I was 16 years old. I loved him so much that I even joined the Johnny Lee Fan Club! In the 1980s, I was a country DJ when Johnny had his biggest radio success. Yes, I played a lot of Johnny Lee.

I also went to see him in concert anytime that I could. He was always such a great entertainer. In 2006, I took my six year old daughter to her first Johnny Lee concert. She had a little toy camera with her, and she walked up to the stage to take his photo. When he saw her, he pulled her up on stage, stopped the show, and posed for a picture with my little girl. After the concert, he gave her his guitar pick. She still has it.

Ten years later, in the spring of 2016, Johnny was taping an episode of 'Larry's Country Diner'. I wrote feature stories for Larry Black's newspaper at that time, and I asked Johnny for an interview. He said, "Sure. Let's go in my dressing room where it is quieter."

As we visited, Johnny was his usual, happy-go-lucky self... until I noticed his rubber bracelet. I asked him, "What does 'Always Remember' mean?"

He looked down at his wrist, and immediately started crying. Just him and me, alone in his dressing room. And he cried, as he told me about his son Johnny.

As he shared his story, I realized that Johnny Lee had lived a truly incredible life. He had lived through the most amazing, highest highs, and the almost unbearable, lowest lows.

I had just completed work on Ronnie McDowell's autobiography, and I asked Johnny, "Have you ever written your life story?"

He said, "I did a book about 25 years ago. But I really wasn't happy with it, and I have lived a lot since then. I would like to do another one."

I knew that was my opening to say, "Hey, I would love to help you!" But I didn't. I didn't say anything. I figured he would want someone else to do his book. I thanked him for the interview, and we both walked out of his dressing room. The entire time, I was kicking myself for not having the self-confidence to at least ask him if I could be involved in his book. The worst he could have said was "No".

A half-hour later, I was backstage watching TV. I sat there saying to myself, "You blew it! You could be working with Johnny Lee! You could have written a great book!"

At that moment, Johnny came and sat down next to me. He said, "Hey man, if you ever wanted to write another book, I'd love for you to do mine."

I have no doubt that it was divine intervention. I looked at Johnny and said, "I would love to."

Johnny Lee says he is "Still lookin' for love."

I'm pretty sure he has already found it.

You can look back at the first photo in this book, as he held his grandson Wyatt for the very first time. He is in love with that tiny baby. That baby's mother, Johnny's daughter Cherish, loves her dad with all her heart. And even her mother Charlene, with whom Johnny had a much-publicized divorce, loves Johnny.

As we worked on this book, I had the pleasure of visiting with so many of Johnny's family members, friends and fellow country artists. And during that time, I have come to the conclusion that Johnny is one of the most loved guys that I have ever met. Everyone who knows him, loves him. His friends all love him. And he loves them. His mother and sisters and brothers all love him. And you can tell that he loves them all just as much.

His fans have loved him for more than 40 years. And he loves his fans even more than they love him. He lives to make them happy. He loves to entertain.

"Still lookin' for love?" Quit looking, Johnny. You found it long ago.

Scot England

Before I close, I want to say thank you to a few people. And I am sure that I'm leaving out many folks. If you are one of those left out, hopefully you'll understand and know that you are in very good company. There are hundreds more who don't see their names here, but I am thankful for each and every one of those people, and you.

I want to give a very special thanks to my mom. She stood by me when I first wanted to get into music.

Thank you to my good friend Mickey Gilley, whom I love like a brother. Without him, I would not be where I am today.

I need to thank Irving Azoff, for recognizing me and my talent.

Thank you to Sandy and David Brokaw, and to Kirt Webster and Webster Public Relations, who do so much work for me.

To my special friends Moe Bandy, T. Graham Brown, T.G. Sheppard and Kelly Lang, Gene Watson, Faron Young, Dottie West, Johnny Paycheck, George Jones, and so many other country music legends.

If you want to keep up on my tour dates or buy one of my CDs, be sure to check out my website at johnnyleemusic.com. You can find my cookbook at that site and if you try any of the recipes, be sure to always use Springer Mountain Farm chicken. I always like to give a plug to Gus Arrendale and his Springer Mountain Farm anytime I can. Gus is such a great supporter of Country Music.

Thank you to Randy Little and all of my friends at PFI Western Store, the home of Boot Daddy! On your way to see me and Mickey in Branson, be sure to stop by PFI in Springfield Missouri. They have been dear friends for years.

A special thanks to Scot England, for helping me write this book.

And I deeply also thank everyone who buys this book. I hope you liked it.

Johnny